INVEST IN YOUR NEST

ADD STYLE, COMFORT, AND VALUE TO YOUR HOME

Barbara K

RODALE

NOTICE

© 2006 by Barbara Kavovit

BOOK DESIGN BY Susan Eugster
ILLUSTRATIONS BY Lisa Henderling

Library of Congress Cataloging-in-Publication Data

Barbara K
    Invest in your nest : add style, comfort, and value to your home / Barbara K
        p.   cm.
    Includes index.
    ISBN-13 978–1–59486–151–2   paperback
    ISBN-10 1–59486–151–X   paperback
    1. Dwellings—Remodeling.   I. Title.
  TH4816.B376   2006
  643'.7—dc22   2006005449

Distributed to the book trade by Holtzbrinck Publishers

2 4 6 8 10 9 7 5 3 1   paperback

*I'm proud to be part of the revolution of women
taking charge of their homes and their lives.
This book is dedicated to all the independent women
of the world and to those who want to be.*

*And to my amazing son, Zachary,
the absolute love and light of my life!*

Contents

!

Acknowledgments

I enjoy inspiring others and am an entrepreneur and pioneer by nature. My business is a good example of this spirit. Through it, I want to start a revolution of women taking charge of their homes and their lives. But I could not have done all that I have accomplished on my own. There are so many people who have helped me from every part of my life: family, friends, and, of course, colleagues and business partners— many of whom I count as friends. I want to thank some of the people from all the different facets of my life, who have helped make barbara k! a reality, and helped me realize so many dreams. They have been there for me and continue to be:

Caryn Kavovit, my sister and friend, and Eric Brunman, her husband and my friend (a great listener!)

Takeesha Banks, my assistant and friend (and how I keep *everything* in my life organized)

Sam Gradess, a friend and investor who was always there to listen to Zach

Brad Rose, attorney at Pryor Cashman Sherman Flynn who has made sure we are well protected!

Holly Gandras, my best friend for 20 years

Richard Russell, mortgage broker at Richland Equity and miracle worker (the best in the business)

Doug Madaio, mortgage broker PIC, who got me the mortgage on my very first house

Pam Marcus, colleague and friend

Paul Davies, friend and former coworker

Karen Kelly, cowriter: Thanks for always getting my thoughts on paper!

Morris L. Reid: Thanks for believing in me and going the distance.

Margot Schupf and Jennifer DeFilippi, editorial director and editor at Rodale Books: Thanks for all your effort, creativity, and dedication.

Lori Augustine, VP of Sales . . . one of the first: Thanks for "sticking."

Testrite International: Thank you to the entire staff both in Asia and the United States.

And to all my investors: Thank you all for believing in me and for your continued support.

A special thanks to all my loyal customers who have bought barbara k! products. Hopefully you, too, are living comfortably in style and making your dreams a reality!

!

About This Book

My goal in life is to be the happiest I can be. The only way to achieve that goal is through learning—aspiring to be the best I can be for myself and my loved ones, and then inspiring others to do the same. I want to share my sense of adventure and the expertise that I've acquired in business and in life, along with my everlasting desire to have fun. All of those qualities ultimately add up to self-confidence and independence, two of the most important tools you need to build a happy life.

If you read my last book, *Room for Improvement* (and if you haven't, run—don't walk—to your local bookstore), you understand how easy and rewarding it is to create your own personalized space at home. Now, in *Invest in Your Nest*, I take that idea a step further. Enjoy renovating and decorating your home, but be smart about where you spend your dollars so you can make a little money in the process, whether you intend to sell or stay put. I often played the board game Monopoly as a kid. I was actually quite good—a neighborhood champion—maybe because I was always playing with other people's money! Investing in your nest is a similar concept. If you already own a home, it's probably your greatest asset, so why not work to improve its value while you add style and comfort? If you don't own a home, buying one is the best way to put your money to work for you. I have been involved in real estate for many years, and I firmly believe it is one of the best investments you can make—financially, emotionally, and for overall quality of life. You can make money while you live in your home by adding style and comfort at the same time—hello, what are you waiting for? When you invest in your nest, you invest in yourself.

Part do-it-yourself (DIY) handbook, part investment guide, part self-help manual, *Invest in Your Nest* is a unique approach to home improvement. In Part 1, I share my own experiences—as a professional contractor and a single mother—in buying, renovating, building, and selling homes, from how to buy a home to how to find the right real estate agent. After that, I walk you through the big picture; that is, I introduce you to the essential inner workings and details of your home. It's not the most glamorous part of home ownership, but if you want to increase your property's value, attending to the plumbing, heating and cooling, windows and doors, flooring, and all the other building basics is where you begin. Finally, Part 3 offers dozens of ideas for enhancing value, comfort, and style, starting with the areas that offer the most bang for your

Imagination, hard work, and an expert construction crew helped build my dream home, pictured here as a work in progress and, on page xv, as it is today.

buck: kitchen, bathrooms, outdoor spaces, and "living" rooms (including the home office, family room, and bedrooms).

To top it all off, the book is filled with easy, "On Your Own" DIY projects that truly increase the value of your home; insider's advice to consider when faced with more complex, "Go to the Pros" jobs; and "Barbara's Best Bet" recommendations for saving money or spending it wisely. "Comfort Zone" tips give you great ideas that will make living in your home even more enjoyable; luckily, these same upgrades appeal to buyers, as well. Whether you decide to lay out a tiled backsplash in the kitchen or hire a licensed electrician for some serious rewiring, I hope the information in this book fills you with confidence and brings joy into your home and your life (and maybe even fattens your wallet).

Go ahead, you can do it! Forget all the reasons you've used to convince yourself that you can't, because I am going to convince you that you can! I feel it, and so should you. You have taken the first step by opening this book. Nothing is an exact science—especially investing in a new home. Everything involves stepping-stones, using what you

learn from each move you make to get to the next step. Don't waste your energy, time, and effort on talking yourself out of it. You are going to need that energy and creativity to buy, build, or renovate your home.

Take it from me, the "you can do it" queen: Unless you try, you will never know what can be, never know what problems you can wrestle with and solve. Solutions will spring from the knowledge you will quickly acquire when you take the plunge. Just do it! I am here to guide you on the way.

Barbara K

PART 1

EXPAND YOUR LIFE WITH REAL ESTATE

I was unlikely to succeed in real estate. Everyone told me I couldn't buy a house. The money I was making, about $40,000 a year, was not enough to buy a $500,000 home. But being told "no" was enough to drive me through a concrete wall! I had a lot of persistence and was determined to own my own home because, first, I realized that I just did not like renting and sharing my summerhouse with other people and, second, I needed a challenge—owning real estate became my mission.

Many people, and women in particular, think about buying a house but don't quite know how to begin. However, you can do it, and why not do it now? Buying a condo or house is always a wise investment, whether it's your primary residence or a property you plan to rent or sell. You can use your investment to upgrade to another bigger, better home, or take the equity you have earned and turn it into money for education, entrepreneurial pursuits, renovation projects, or retirement. Owning your own place opens the door to endless possibilities.

It doesn't take a lot of money or the best-paying job to qualify for a mortgage and then add incredible style, comfort, and value to your home. You just need the right tools, a bit of enthusiasm, and a positive attitude. If circumstances in your life have been holding you back, there is no time like the present to get creative. There are so many deals to be made, so many locations that can be developed, so many songs to be sung (I love to sing while I work; Velvet Revolver is my favorite band!). But enough about singing; it's time to get started.

In Chapter 1, The Big Buy, I give you basic information about buying a house, whether it's a small urban condo or a big spread in the country. I've created a format that is easy to understand and anticipates a lot of the questions you may have about getting a mortgage, making an offer, and moving in. I use that same format in Chapter 2, The Essential Sell, to help you ready your house for sale so you get the best price possible. Then you can buy an even better nest to invest in!

!

CHAPTER 1

The Big Buy

Every time I pull in my driveway my heart starts pounding because I can't believe I actually live in my dream house (of the moment), never mind the fact that if I ever decide to sell it, the equity I have built in the house will allow me to retire to almost any part of our beautiful country. It all started when I took the plunge and bought my first house.

Buying a house is probably the biggest purchase you will ever make, but it's not out of your reach. It's a matter of persistence and focus. I used sheer determination along with every penny I had saved since I was a teenager to buy my first property. I wasn't even sure how I was going to pay the mortgage once the deal was done (making $40,000 a year wasn't going to cut it). Yet having a place to call my own was so important to me that I was determined to find a way.

It was the summer of 1995. Like so many other young people, I was sharing a house at the beach with 10 other girls and guys. And it was costing me about $2,000 over the 3 summer months to rent a house that I had access to only every other weekend. And when I *was* there, I'd get up in the morning and wend my way around visiting strag-

3

glers who were sleeping on the staircase and floor. Yuck! One morning I had had enough and I told my friends I was going out to buy a house. They looked at me like I had five heads, but they underestimated me. That same weekend I saw a three-bed-room, two-bathroom ranch house on a large, 2-acre lot in the town of Wainscott, New York. I made an offer negotiated through a real estate agent and it was accepted. I was on my way.

I had enough cash to put down about $50,000 on the house (I had been saving since I was 13), but no money for closing costs. Contrary to common wisdom, you don't need 20 percent of the price as a down payment, and sometimes you can buy a house with no money down—but more on that later. I extended the closing date long enough that I was able to save a little money for the closing costs. Once I closed on the house, my then-husband and I began working on an addition to make the house renter-friendly. I brought in a surveyor to determine the boundaries of the property. Then I hired an architect and a team of guys to add three more bedrooms and two additional bathrooms to the house. By this time it was spring, the beginning of the renting season—the right time to put an ad for tenants in the local paper. As the paint was drying on the additional bedrooms and baths, the summer of 1996 rolled around and we were all ready for the tenants I had lined up and the mortgage I had to pay each month.

The man I'd bought the property from told me that when he originally bought the land, he had combined two separate parcels into one certificate of occupancy. That meant it might be possible for me to convert it back into separate lots so I could eventually build another house on the second lot. And that's exactly what I did 2 years later, when I built the house I live in now! I sold the original house for a substantial profit on what I had paid for it and put into it, and I also had a separate building lot that I owned outright, free and clear of a mortgage.

With the money I had earned on the original property, I was able to pay the mortgage and build up enough equity to take out another loan to build another house on a lot up the road. Once that house was built, I sold it, again at a profit. So as you can see, one initial, well-planned real estate investment can quickly and significantly improve your financial status.

So, let's get going and buy a house!

YOU CAN AFFORD IT!

You're ready to make the investment of a lifetime. Obviously, you could delay to save more money before you buy, but why wait if you don't have to? I'm the kind of person who just goes after what she wants when she wants it. I don't like to wait for opportunities to come to me. Sometimes you have to create your own opportunities.

KNOW YOUR CREDIT SCORE

The most important part of qualifying for a mortgage isn't how much of a down payment you can make, it's how good your credit score is. The better your credit, the more easily you can secure a mortgage loan, even without a fat bank account or a high-paying job. The first and most important action you should take is to get your credit report from each of the three major credit bureaus, Experian, Equifax, and TransUnion (see page 8 for contact information). You have to get all three reports because the companies and utilities that extend you credit don't report to all three bureaus. The result is that each consumer has three credit reports with three different sets of information. You can access the reports for free at least once a year. If you find errors and report them (see below for details), you can get a revised report for free.

Your credit score is based on the information in the credit report. In the simplest terms, the score indicates how likely you will be to pay back a loan in full and on time. According to Steven Burman, president of Credit Advocates and an expert credit counselor, it reflects your credit history, how much debt you currently carry (called outstanding debt), how much debt you're already approved to carry in the future (add up the credit limits on your credit cards for the answer), how long your credit history is, and how timely you are in paying bills. The higher the number, the better your credit is, ranging from a low of 300 to a perfect score of 850. Do everything you can to improve your score—it's even more important than saving money, in my opinion! Why? Because the higher your score, the better the interest rate you will get. If you have a very high score, you may even be able to buy a house with no money down.

IMPROVE YOUR CREDIT RATING

Steve says that you have to take personal responsibility for your credit, and I agree. The first time many people see their credit reports is when they are about to purchase a home or a car. Because it can take about 3 months (and sometimes much longer) to change a credit score, if the score is wrong or low at that time, it could be too late to fix it. You could lose that fabulous apartment! Don't let that happen—start changing your score *today*. Here are six proven ways to improve your score:

1. Check and correct your credit history

Thirty-five percent of your score comes from your credit history, according to Steve. Unfortunately, 70 percent of credit reports contain errors—mistakes that can adversely impact your score! Mistakes range from the misspelling of names, to reporting wrong addresses or places of employment, to confusing the accounts of people with the same name, to including outdated information. You can and should report errors to each of the credit bureaus since they do not share information. You can file disputes by phone or by mail, but you may find that it is most convenient to dispute errors online. Once the credit bureaus receive a dispute, they have 30 days to investigate. If they cannot verify the information in that time, it is deleted or corrected by default. Once you dispute information, the onus is on them to prove it. If your payment was late once or twice and the creditor reported it to the credit bureau, you can ask the retailer or credit card company to issue a letter of correction. For example, many retail stores would prefer to keep your business by issuing a correction than lose it by refusing to. Always follow up on promised corrections by rechecking your credit report. If some of the accounts on your report are old and closed, tell the credit bureau that you don't recognize them. They will investigate, find that you are not a customer, and remove them. It's best if your credit report lists only active accounts. Even when some of the accounts are closed, having dozens of them may make lenders assume that you are not a stable credit risk.

2. Pay down high balances

The amounts you owe on revolving credit accounts are responsible for 30 percent of your score. Steve says the fastest way to improve your credit rating is to pay down balances. After he advised one client to use all of his available cash to pay down his credit card bills, the client's credit score went up by 100 points. Keep revolving credit accounts under 30 percent of the available limit. For example, if your credit card limit is $10,000, keep the balance under $3,000. High balances adversely affect credit ratings. Plus, credit card debt is expensive to carry. Some cards charge up to 24 percent interest on unpaid balances. Are the designer jeans and fur jacket really worth that? Pay off your credit cards! You can also negotiate with your credit card company to reduce or eliminate interest charges and sometimes even reduce what you owe.

3. Make history with your credit

It's good to have some activity and history on the account. "Many people think closing accounts will make their credit look better, but it depends," says Steve. "Look at the accounts you are closing and keep the oldest one. Length of credit history counts for 15 percent of your total score."

4. Think twice about new credit

When you open a new credit card account, the creditor makes an inquiry to one of the credit bureaus to evaluate your history. The number of recently opened accounts and credit inquiries accounts for 10 percent of your score. (Note that checking your own credit report doesn't count as an inquiry, however.) "If you start applying for loans at an auto dealership or a bank and each one does an inquiry, it's a negative," says Steve. When a store sends you a sales pitch saying you're preapproved for credit, resist the temptation to fill out the application form. One credit card is all you really need. At any rate, closing an account doesn't mean it automatically disappears from your credit report. You have to ask them to remove it. Better yet . . .

5. Pay with cash

Using debit cards and cash are good ways to control your debt (and therefore maintain a great credit score).

6. Pay all your bills on time

Late payments can have a substantial negative impact on your score. For example, you can raise your score by as much as 20 points simply by paying bills on time for 1 month!

For more information on improving your credit rating, visit the Federal Trade Commission's credit repair page at www.ftc.gov/bcp/conline/pubs/credit/repair.htm. To dispute information in a credit report, here is how to contact the credit bureaus:

Equifax Information Services, LLC
Disclosure Department
PO Box 740241
Atlanta, GA 30374
800-685-1111
www.equifax.com

Experian
475 Anton Boulevard
Costa Mesa, CA 92626
or
955 American Lane
Schaumburg, IL 60173
888-397-3742
www.experian.com

TransUnion LLC
PO Box 1000
Chester, PA 19022
800-888-4213
www.transunion.com

Annual Credit Report Request Service
PO Box 105281
Atlanta, GA 30348-5281
877-322-8228
www.annualcreditreport.com

Annualcreditreport.com is the official site that helps consumers obtain the free credit reports they are entitled to annually, as required by law.

DEFINE WHAT YOU WANT

My eyes light up and my adrenaline flares whenever I look at real estate. Figuring out what kind of place you want is so much fun. Sometimes you see a place you love right away. Sometimes it takes a while. If you take the time to think about what you want and how long you plan to stay in your home before you start looking, you will be more focused. Before I found the Wainscott house, the real estate agent showed me eight houses that ranged in style from modern to quaint and traditional. Every one of them had features I liked, but the lot and layout of the house I bought had many of the qualities I knew I wanted. For example, the lot was large enough and the home's floor plan was basic enough that I knew I could expand with relative ease. It doesn't cost anything to look at houses and create an image in your mind of what you truly want to own.

It's a good idea to write down everything you'd like your home to have. A list keeps you focused. Make a wish list of everything you want. What's your lifestyle? What's important to you? For example, I love light and could not live in a dark house with limited exposure to the sun. I would rather have a smaller house with bright, sunny rooms than a bigger place with small windows and little natural light. What about house style? Are you modern or do you love traditional? Or do you feel open to almost any style?

Location is important, too. When I went looking for my first house, I knew I wanted a house in a great location that was convenient for shopping and close to the beach. Also, more important, I wanted it to be on the "right" side of the highway. The house I bought was close to a bus stop so visitors could get from New York City to my house very easily. There was also a good fish market that had a friendly owner within walking distance, not to mention the beach!

You might get a good deal on a house in a neighborhood that's "up and coming," meaning that the boundaries of a better neighborhood or town are being pushed farther out to include other streets, sections, or towns. An indication that a neighborhood is on the upswing is when you see a lot of home improvement activity and new construction. If many people are putting money into fixing up their homes, it means they see value in their property and plan on staying for a while or selling at a profit.

Up-and-coming areas may be farther from your place of work, have fewer services and amenities (such as supermarkets and playgrounds), and have a lower-ranking school system than established neighborhoods. Do those things matter to you, or can you predict future improvement in those areas? Is traveling a bit farther to buy food or see a movie worth it to you in exchange for a great house at a good price, which will only increase in value as the services and amenities eventually make inroads into the area?

Think about how much farther you are willing to walk or drive—and then actually take the drive or walk from that neighborhood during the week, at night, and on the weekend to see if it's doable. If you're searching in a city and use public transportation to get around, try commuting from that location one morning. How bad is it? Can you handle the trip twice a day, five days a week? If not, you'd better shift your search to another area. How is the location in the evening? Would you be comfortable traveling home alone after working late or dancing the night away in a club?

If you simply must have a house in an established and popular location, it will cost more. You may have to cut back on the size of the home or the features it includes and add space or amenities after you move in. That's not a bad plan if it buys you a house in a great neighborhood. One thing to keep in mind, however, is that if a location is really desirable, you may have to make serious concessions on your wish list or be ready to roll up your sleeves and put sweat equity into a fixer-upper. I happen to love fixer-uppers and would buy one any day of the week. I always say, buy the least expensive house in the most expensive neighborhood!

You can also buy a new place or one that

barbara's best bet

FIXER-UPPERS

When I see a house that needs help, I immediately get excited and see dollar signs. A house that needs work is like money in your pocket, because as soon as you make even one improvement on a needy house, your equity in it—as well as its resale value—increases. In fact, unlike most people, I stay away from renovated houses. Why pay someone else for work you can do to your exact specifications yourself? Don't be afraid of work, which can make you money at the same time.

has not yet been built. Preconstruction condos and houses have a financial advantage, too, because the time it takes to build them is time during which your deposit is working for you in escrow. Once an apartment house or development is completed, the price almost without exception goes up. Look at it this way: You have not done a thing and yet the value of your house and your equity have increased!

Another option is to buy a piece of land and build a house on it. You can also buy a total wreck of a house, tear it down, and start over. Every community has laws and regulations concerning demolition and rebuilding, so before you take that plunge do your homework and find out what the permit and paperwork requirements are. Either way, when you build rather than buy a ready-made house, you need to get a construction loan, which is different from a mortgage.

These days, a land loan often can be converted into a construction loan, which then can be converted into a mortgage when the house is built. The advantage of these convertible loans is that there's one loan application and one loan closing. The lender finances the construction of the home and, when it's ready for occupancy, the loan converts into a mortgage. You don't have a lot of negotiating power on the interest rate for the permanent financing because decisions about the terms of the loan are made when you close prior to construction. You have to pay a fee when converting a construction loan to a mortgage (about $350), but you may be able to get a better interest rate on the mortgage. Talk to a mortgage broker about alternatives. More on mortgages is to come, but first here's a word on finding that dream home with the right real estate agent.

go to the pros

FIND THE RIGHT REAL ESTATE AGENT

Once you have determined what you want in a house, you have to start hunting and that generally begins with selecting a real estate agent. It's possible to find a house on your own, but a real estate agent saves you time in the long run by pre-evaluating houses so you don't waste too much time viewing properties that are off the mark. Even though finding an agent might seem pretty straightforward, not all real estate agents are created equal. You have to find one who is going to take the time to get to know you and understand your needs so he or she can sell you the right house, not just any house.

Who are these people?

Most real estate agents work for the seller, which is why the seller pays a commission to the agent when his or her house is sold. Some represent buyers and others even represent both buyer and seller. This information should be disclosed to you right away. If it is not, ask. You'll want to know whose side the agent is on. Just because an agent works for the seller doesn't mean that using an agent doesn't cost you anything—the commission the seller pays is built into the price you pay for the house. As a buyer, you can work with more than one agent if you like, but all agents will have access to almost any house you're interested in, even if it's not in that agency's database, because they are part of the local multiple listing service (MLS).

Where do I find them?

It seems like there is a real estate office on every corner of every city and town in America! Recommendations from friends are always helpful, but if you are looking for a home in a new area, it's best to visit a few agencies and talk to the agents.

What kind of training and certification do they need?

A real estate agent should have a state license to practice—and it should be displayed prominently in his or her office. To get a license, an agent must complete a course of study and pass a state exam.

What else do I need to know?

As a buyer you want the agent to understand what you're looking for—bring your "must have" list with you. Then, make an appointment with the agent to see several properties. I looked at more than eight houses the first time I bought a house. If you can't find a house you like after walking through more than 10, it might be time to reevaluate either your must-have list or your agent. Maybe he or she doesn't understand what you are looking for and you should find a new agent. Don't be bullied into a sale. If you think a real estate agent is pressuring you, walk away. In addition, look for an agent who is familiar with the area and willing to take the time to show you the local restaurants, grocery stores, scenic routes and shortcuts, schools, and playgrounds and parks for children and pets.

UNDERSTAND THE LANGUAGE OF MORTGAGES

Once you have found the land, house, or condo of your dreams, you will most likely need to apply for a mortgage. There are different kinds of mortgages, each representing a different way of financing the purchase of a house. Talk to your mortgage broker or lender to figure out which one is best for you. Here are the two most common types:

Fixed rate. This type has both a fixed term (usually 15 or 30 years) and a fixed interest rate, both determined at the start of the mortgage. The monthly payment of principal and interest doesn't change during the term of the mortgage. A fixed-rate mortgage is a good idea if you plan to live in the house for more than 5 years and interest rates are predicted to go up. A 30-year mortgage means you'll have lower monthly payments, but over the long run, you'll be paying more for your house because you'll be paying more interest. With a 15-year mortgage, the monthly bill will be higher, but you'll end up paying less for your house because it will be paid off in a shorter period of time.

Adjustable rate. The interest rate on your mortgage will be raised or lowered according to the current interest rate. The monthly amount for your principal and interest payment will go up or down with these rate changes. If rates go down, you win. If they go up, you can lose. This type of mortgage is best if rates are low and you don't expect to stay in the house for more than a few years. I took out a 30-year adjustable mortgage on my first house because I wanted lower monthly payments and I did not expect to own the house for long.

$

barbara's best bet

GET PREAPPROVED

Preapproval gives you a lot of leverage when buying a house. The seller sees it as an advantage because he or she knows you are a serious buyer able to close the deal very quickly because you've already secured the loan. To get preapproved, you provide the same information to the lender that you would if you applied for a mortgage after making an offer. Your income, credit history (and credit score), debts, and assets will be verified. The lender then issues a letter stating that your mortgage is approved for up to a certain dollar amount for a certain period of time. Once you've been preapproved for a mortgage, avoid taking on any substantial new debt and make timely payments on all of your existing debts. Otherwise, you risk damaging your credit rating in the middle of the buying process. If the lender charges a preapproval fee, negotiate to have it refunded at the closing.

go to the pros

SELECT A MORTGAGE BROKER

You can get a mortgage directly from a bank, a mortgage company, or a credit union, but I believe you can get the best deal on a mortgage through a mortgage broker.

Who are these people?

A mortgage broker is an independent or "third party" person or company who, for a fee, finds favorable loan terms for a buyer. A broker has the ability to look at many possible deals and streamline the application and approval process.

Where do I find them?

Most likely, your real estate agent or attorney can recommend a trustworthy mortgage broker. Otherwise, contact your state's mortgage broker association.

What kind of training and certification do they need?

Federal laws and enforcement agencies regulate mortgage banking and brokers. Specific education and experience requirements vary by state, but no matter where they practice, a broker should have a college degree or its equivalent, several years of experience in the profession, and access to a variety of lending institutions.

What else do I need to know?

First ask for details on each potential loan:

- Is the rate fixed or adjustable? What is the loan's annual percentage rate (APR)? Expressed as a yearly rate, this includes the interest rate, points, broker fees, and any credit charges you may have to pay.

- How do the points translate into dollars? A *point* is a fee paid to the lender or broker for the loan. Ask each potential lender for a quote in dollars (rather than just the number of points) so you'll know how much you will have to pay at the closing.

- Is private mortgage insurance (PMI) required? If you put down less than 20 percent, lenders generally require you to purchase PMI to protect them in case you fail to repay the loan. Find out the exact monthly cost of PMI and how long you will be required to carry it.

Once you find the best possible terms, ask the broker for a written rate lock. It should stipulate the interest rate, how long the lock-in will last, and the number of points to be paid. Locking in protects you from a rate increase if interest rates go up while your loan is being processed.

MAKE AN OFFER!

Congratulations! You've found a house you love. But hold on! Before you submit an offer, visit the house at night and on the weekend. Walk around the neighborhood. Make sure it's comfortable and quiet (or lively and loud, if that's what you're after). Take a close look at the adjacent houses. Do the neighbors maintain their homes? Do they have bamboo or other invasive plants growing in the backyard? (I once walked away from a deal after discovering that the backyard of the house next to the one I was considering was full of bamboo that would eventually come over to my side. I knew from experience that it would be nearly impossible to control if the neighbors weren't willing to eradicate it.) If everything checks out, don't show your enthusiasm to the seller or the seller's agent. They can and will use that information to get more money from you.

Before making an offer, ask your agent for a comparative market analysis (CMA). This informal report lists the addresses of recently sold homes in the same neighborhood, along with the date of the sale, the price, and the number of bedrooms and bathrooms. You can find similar information on Web sites that list recent sales in your areas. To find such sites, use "recent real estate sales" or "real estate sales" as key words when searching with a search engine, such as Google. Your offer should be comparable to those selling prices, which may not be the same as the seller's asking price.

If you make an offer and the seller accepts it, insist that the contract include two escape clauses: a financing (or mortgage) contingency and an inspection contingency. If for some reason you can't get a mortgage, the financing contingency releases you from the contract and guarantees that you will get back any deposit money you put down on the house (called *earnest money*).

The inspection contingency will release you from the contract and ensure the return of your deposit if a licensed professional inspector finds any damage or structural flaws in the house during a thorough inspection. Usually, you can also opt to use the inspection contingency to negotiate for the seller to undertake repairs to the house or for a lower selling price without repairs. There are different types of inspection contingencies; work with your agent to put the type you want into the written offer you make on the house.

Your offer could be turned down because the seller wants more money; make a counteroffer if you really love the house! Be prepared to make a "best and final offer"— the most you are willing to pay for the house. If the seller still says no, remember that there are always other houses for sale.

go to the pros

WORK WITH A HOME INSPECTOR

Any offer you make should always be contingent upon a satisfactory whole-house inspection. Inspections disclose defects in the property that could affect its safety, livability, or resale value.

Who are these people?

An inspector is someone who looks at a home's basic structural features and reports on them to you in writing. They usually charge a flat fee for the service, typically from $500 to $1,000. Prices vary by region and by home.

What kind of training and certification do they need?

An inspector should have several years of experience and be certified by the American Society of Home Inspectors. Ask the inspector if he or she has errors and omissions insurance, too. This gives you some level of protection should the inspector overlook or forget to mention something important.

How long does an inspection take and what happens?

Depending on the size of the property, an inspection should take 2 to 4 hours. Carve out some time to accompany him or her on the inspection so you can take notes on everything from how to open the chimney flue to what size filter the furnace takes. The inspector will look at all the basic structural features of the house, including the following:

Foundation. Is there evidence of cracks, shifting, or excessive moisture?

General construction. How good is the quality of the general construction?

Exterior. If the property is a house, does it need exterior repairs or maintenance? What is the approximate age of the roof? What is the estimated remaining life of the roof? Is the condition good? What about landscaping? Have mature trees or shrubs close to the house caused damage to the home's foundation?

Pests. Is there any indication of pests, such as rodents, termites, carpenter ants, or other insects?

Attached structures. What is the condition of any attached structure (for example, a shed, deck, or garage)?

Plumbing. What is the overall condition of the plumbing system? Is there evidence of leaks or water pressure problems?

Electrical. Do any dangerous electrical situations or code violations exist? What is the electrical output capacity (especially in older homes)?

Heating and cooling systems. What are the ages of these systems? Are they adequate for the size of the house?

Interior. Do doors and windows open and close properly? Are floors firm and level?

Kitchen. Are appliances functioning properly? Is the plumbing, including the dishwasher connection, in good repair?

Baths. Is the floor solid? Is there evidence of old or new water leaks?

Attic and basement. Are the floor and ceiling joists solid? Is there any indication of water damage or mold?

Radon testing. Is there an unacceptably high level of radon in the home? Homes all over the United States have been found to have some level of radon, according to the US Environmental Protection Agency. An elevated rate is considered to be 4 or more picocuries per liter. Check the EPA's Web site (www.epa.gov/radon) for more information.

PURCHASING HOME-OWNER'S INSURANCE

You're almost done, but before you seal the deal you need to show proof of insurance on the property. An independent insurance agent sells policies from a variety of insurers and can help you find the best policy. The best policies cover the cost of replacing the home and its contents in case of fire, theft, or other disasters—even terrorist attacks (in New York City, for example, many insurers now offer terrorism riders). You can also purchase riders for flood and hurricane damage, which may be especially important if you live in a region of the country that is prone to these events.

Whatever risks you choose to address, make sure you insure the house for an amount that reflects a realistic rebuilding cost. This differs from the market value of your house—it is the real cost of replacement, not what you can sell your house for. Some insurance pros estimate that 59 percent of American homes are underinsured by about 22 percent. You don't want to come up short in the unlikely event that you have to rebuild.

If you live in a landmark home that has a lot of expensive original woodwork, for example, replacing even one paneled room or a fancy staircase could cost tens of thousands of dollars. Do you want to cover that with insurance? The policy will be more expensive if you do, but it could be worth it. Or, you may live in an architecturally important newer home. Some modern homes built in the 1950s, for example, have a design pedigree that should be protected. On average, an inland home can cost about $150 per square foot to rebuild, while a luxury or waterfront home or one built into a steep hill can cost $200 to $500 per square foot to rebuild. Houses in upscale urban areas, even if they are on flat land, can cost more than $250 per square foot to replace. A contractor familiar with your area should be able to give you an estimate of replacement costs for insurance purposes.

Find out from the insurer what you can do to decrease your premium. Depending on where you live, installing alarm systems or storm shutters can help bring down the cost of insurance. You may also get a discount on your home-owner's policy if you already have an automobile policy or other coverage with the same provider.

You also have to evaluate the worth of what's inside your home, including furniture, electronic equipment, collections, and other valuables. Some insurers will value your home's contents at half the value of rebuilding the home, but that may not be adequate for you. Instead, make a video of the inside of your home and your important possessions. Keep it and any receipts or written appraisals for big-ticket items like artwork or fancy electronics in another, safe location (such as a safe-deposit box). E-mail a list of your valuables along with photos of them and any electronic documentation of receipts to a friend who can make a copy and keep the electronic files safe.

But don't overdo it when insuring your precious possessions. Insuring an engagement ring as part of a home-owner's policy can price that policy out of your reach. By the time you finish paying the premiums over a period of just a few years, well, you could have bought yourself a new diamond ring! If you want to, you can insure certain valuables individually as "floaters" because they can leave the home. Your broker will probably recommend a separate underwriter for such important items.

If you own certain breeds of dog, such as the pit bull, that have a reputation for being vicious, you may find it difficult to buy home-owner's insurance or to renew an existing policy if the dog bites or harms a person or their pet. It may seem unfair, but it's a growing trend among insurers.

Finally, a policy with a high deductible may be your best bet. A high deductible gets you smaller premiums and a smoother claims process.

CLOSE THE DEAL

I delayed closing the deal on my first house for as long as I could. During that time, I was able to save enough money to cover the closing costs. Also, since closing then occurred during the summer rental season, I was able to collect enough rental income to make my mortgage payments for the year.

Closing is the process you go through to finalize the deal you made to buy the house, assume ownership, and take possession of the property. Closing procedures vary from region to region. In some areas, the buyer, seller, and real estate agents all attend. In other areas, only the buyer and his or her agent attend, along with the closing agent. The closing happens in a lawyer's, title company's, or escrow company's office. The seller's attorney prepares the deed and coordinates all the other paperwork with the buyer's attorney or closing agent. I used to attend closings, but then I learned that you can give your lawyer "power of attorney" and need not attend.

There is a lot of paperwork involved in a real estate transaction. Get your pen ready! Here is a list of the common documents that are prepared for a closing:

☐ Settlement statement

☐ Contract

☐ Loan papers (for the buyer) giving the monthly payment amount, which includes real estate taxes

☐ Title insurance (from the buyer)

☐ Proof of home-owner's insurance (from the buyer)

☐ Title or deed

☐ Down payment and closing costs (from the buyer)

☐ Payoff for any existing mortgage

☐ Funds available to the seller upon recording the new deed

BEYOND THE DOWN PAYMENT: CLOSING COSTS

Closing costs are expenses associated with the loan you take out to buy property. Most but not all of these costs must be paid on the day you finalize your purchase. Luckily, you will have a fairly good idea of how much you will have to set aside for closing costs because the Real Estate Settlement Procedures Act (RESPA) requires that lenders and mortgage brokers give you what is called a *good faith estimate* of the loan-related expenses due at the closing. Here is a list of the fees most commonly included in closing costs:

A loan origination fee covers the lender's costs of processing the loan. Measured in "points," each one of which represents 1 percent of the loan amount, the fee varies among lenders.

A loan discount or "discount point" is a charge imposed by the lender or broker in exchange for lowering the interest rate on the loan. Each point costs 1 percent of the loan amount and lowers the rate by 0.125 percent.

Appraisal fees pay for an appraisal report, which the bank or lender requires to establish the property's worth before issuing you a loan to buy it.

A credit report fee pays for the reports the lender uses to check your credit history.

Title search and title insurance fees ensure that the property is not subject to liens or other problems. Some states require you to hire a lawyer to conduct a title search; others allow you to hire a title search company to do this work.

Notary and recording fees may be charged by the closing agent to have loan documents notarized and the new deed recorded in your community's public record.

A lender's inspection fee is charged when you build a home or buy a house or apartment that is under construction. The fee covers the cost of the routine inspections the lender requires to monitor construction and then release funds as work progresses.

The fee for home inspection is considered a closing cost, even though you pay for it before the actual closing date. Specialized inspection costs, such as radon tests and pest inspections, also fall into this category.

Depending on the location of the property you're purchasing, some of these fees may not apply, or there may be additional fees. For example, if you are buying a house in a private community, annual dues may be owed at closing. So be sure your lender or mortgage broker includes a comprehensive list of fees when he or she gives you a good faith estimate.

*Okay—you've bought your house and settled in, and maybe you're
already itching to fix it up a little and sell it at a profit.
I'm all for it. Turn the page and we'll get started.*

!

CHAPTER 2

The Essential Sell

I am always into the next best thing—or, rather, house. Every time I build, renovate, or move in to a home, I think about how I can increase its value so I can eventually sell and upgrade. I know the old saying "Home is where the heart is," but I say you can put your heart into a new home and also have a lot more money in the bank. This is what it is all about! Are you up for the challenge? You have to sell at least once to get the feel for it. Then maybe you'll get on a roll and want to do it again and again!

I use different approaches when it comes to business, but only one way of thinking when it comes to real estate: Buy it and improve it whenever you have the chance. It translates into tangible financial worth—not like stocks or bonds. You can do many things with a house or condo that you can't with a financial instrument, such as live in it, expand it, renovate it, and sell it. Therefore, you can enjoy it while you are planning and strategizing about your next steps to improve it or buy more property or sell something else you already own.

Putting a house on the market is as exciting as buying one, but it can also be more nerve-racking. What happens if no one bites? What happens if the house languishes on the market? What should you do if you get more than one offer? Who is the real estate agent working for, anyway? How do you prepare a house for a good sale? How do you make sure the agent is pricing the house fairly? Don't worry—I'll give you the lowdown on everything from preparing your pad for a quick, profitable sale to dealing with agents and fielding offers.

PRESENTATION PERFECT

The good news is that there are ways to make the selling process less stressful. Plus, there are many simple, inexpensive or cost-free tricks of the trade you can employ to make your house more appealing to buyers so you'll get top dollar.

First things first: If you can afford to do so, address major issues *before* you list your house. You will always get your money back with big repairs. For example, if part or all of your home's roof needs replacing, do it before your house hits the market. Have plumbing or electrical problems taken care of as well (see Chapter 3 for tips on hiring plumbers and electricians). Once completed, the renovations can be marketed as "new roof," "updated electric," "modern plumbing and heating," and so on, all of which are premium selling points.

After you've taken care of the major matters, work on creating the feeling of a desirable lifestyle in your home. It's amazing how much little details count. Buying a house is as much an emotional decision as a practical one—and often emotion overtakes logic. You want buyers to look around your house and immediately feel that they could move right in and start living the fabulous lifestyle you've been enjoying there.

STAGING

Making cosmetic changes to your house to make it appealing to a variety of buyers is called *staging*. For several thousand dollars you can hire a professional stager or project manager and his or her team. But why do that when you can do it yourself?

Depending on the state and condition of your house, as well as how many extra hands you have helping, cleaning and staging can take from a week to a month. I break home preparations into two sets of activities, the Three Ds and the Three Rs—that is, declutter, depersonalize, and deodorize, then repair, replace, and repaint.

The Three Ds

A clutter-free, scrupulously clean house is essential when selling, especially if you don't have the latest kitchen appliances or fancy flooring or other finishes. If a house is tidy and well organized it shows well. Buyers will often feel they can at least move in and live with the less-than-modern kitchen or un-spa-like bath for a while.

Declutter. The first thing you should do is sort through your possessions and hold a major garage or stoop sale. Search closets, storage spaces, cupboards, and drawers for everything that is no longer useful to you but in good enough condition to be functional for someone else. For example, small appliances, furniture, children's clothing, and toys are all excellent candidates. While you're at it, throw away items that are broken and beyond repair, including torn or worn-out clothes. If you need to toss a ton of stuff, you can rent a small to large Dumpster for $150 to $500 a day, depending on how much rubbish it holds. Containers range in size from 2 to 40 yards (which is how garbage is measured). Donate unsold serviceable items to local charities and recycle old electronic and computer equipment. Next, clear rooms of excess furniture you don't want to part with. Space equals dollars in a buyer's mind, so anything you can do to create the illusion of lots of it will be profitable. Don't store the overflow in your garage, basement, or attic, because buyers like to see these areas open and clean. Instead, rent a storage space for a month or stow gear in a friend's or family member's garage or basement.

Give each room a clean, streamlined, upscale-hotel-suite appearance. Bedrooms should have a bed, one or two nightstands, a dresser, and a comfortable chair if there's room. Add pillows and throws for a cozy, lived-in look. Closets should be organized and airy, not stuffed to the rafters. Jam-packed closets make buyers think storage space in your home is limited (and, while that might be true, you don't want to let on!). The living and family rooms should contain a sofa and chairs, coffee table, side tables, and a rug. TVs and electronic equipment are fine, but they should be stored neatly on a shelf or in a cabinet. Kitchen and bathroom countertops should be free of all extraneous items. Small appliances, such as a toaster oven or coffeemaker in the kitchen and a hair dryer in the bathroom, should be kept to a minimum or, preferably, stored out of sight.

Pick up stray toys, bicycles, and gardening equipment outside your home and place them neatly in a garage or shed or under a deck. Get stuff off the floor by using bungee cords to attach it to the garage or basement walls. Keep the lawn mowed and garden beds tidy. Replace dead flowers with fresh plants.

Depersonalize. Take down family pictures everywhere but in the bedrooms. Ditto for sports trophies, refrigerator magnets, and children's artwork. When you're selling a house, you want buyers to imagine themselves living in it, and seeing your personal memorabilia in every room makes that difficult. I think having a few well-chosen family photos in the bedrooms is nice, but they should be off-limits in other rooms of the house. Remember, it's only temporary!

Deodorize. Don't just clean your house—scrub it until it sparkles. Clean in places you don't look and can't even see into. For example, clean under the sink and behind the toilet in all the bathrooms. Clean the insides of kitchen cabinets and, yes, even the refrigerator (buyers open everything—didn't you when you were house hunting?). Hire a professional to clean carpets and upholstery. You may not be selling your couch along with your house, but something as seemingly innocuous as a less than pristine sofa will signal to the buyer that the entire house is not well maintained. Wash draperies and window treatments, including blinds and shades. Get rid of pet and cigarette or cigar odors. You don't want buyers to remember your house by its smell! Plus, being able to advertise your home as a "pet-free" (or at least "pet-odor free") and "smoke-free" environment is a big selling point.

The Three Rs

Repair. Now is the time to tackle your household to-do list. When buyers see a hole in the drywall, a garden bed filled with weeds and dead plants, or a banister with missing posts, they see more work for themselves. They may also assume that there are bigger problems waiting to be discovered. They may not walk away from your house, but the work you neglect to do will be reflected in a lower offer. You want buyers to walk into your house and feel like they could move right in.

Replace. There may be items in your house that are simply beyond repair. Replace as many of them as you can for a 100 percent return on your investment, if not more. I'm talking about cosmetic surgery here, not gut renovation. Replacement fixtures should be in keeping with the style of your house and appeal to the market you are after without getting too taste-specific. Keep it simple. But if you can, add more shower-heads to your shower—that's a relatively inexpensive addition that is worth double what you spend.

Put the most money into the kitchen and bathrooms, even if you are just making cosmetic changes for a quick sale. If your kitchen countertops are old, new ones can make the kitchen look fresh again. If appliances are old and worn, replace them with modern ones; you don't have to buy the expensive brands for resale. If your bathroom vanities are dated, replace them. New faucets and light fixtures—even inexpensive models—can create a luxurious (valuable, in other words) feeling in a freshly scrubbed, clutter-free kitchen and bathroom.

Repaint. Painting is a time-honored way to brighten up any room. It's inexpensive and easy to apply. If your impulse is to paint all the rooms a stark white, don't. White expanses are difficult to keep clean and make rooms feel cold. There are plenty of off-the-shelf neutral colors you can choose from—off-whites and creamy beiges appeal to the greatest number of people. In the kitchen, consider giving a fresh coat of crisp white paint to dated and dark cabi-

$

barbara's best bet

THINK INSIDE THE BOX

Repair costs, even small ones, have a way of adding up. When you sell your house, you can deduct what you spent on improving it from the profits, which decreases your tax bill. I can't tell you how many times I've needed to refer back to receipts that I'd somehow misplaced. Well, finally I got smart and figured out a way to keep all those papers in one place without having to start a filing system (boring!). Keep all receipts and records in a dedicated, accessible box. You can sort through them later. Having everything in one place is more important than having each piece of paper filed correctly.

nets. Paint trim a glossy white unless it is stained wood, in which case you should clean it with an oil-based wood cleaner to freshen it before you paint the surrounding walls.

FIND THE BEST BUYER

Once you put your house on the market, prepare for an onslaught of potential buyers—and welcome it with open arms, because that's what's going to get you the big bucks. Yes, it is a lot of work to keep your house staged and red-carpet ready all the time, but that's why you did the decluttering and scrubbing before it went on the market. If your house is tidy to begin with, it is easier to maintain that level of order throughout the selling process.

There are two ways to sell a house: with or without a real estate agent. Both ways have advantages, but most sellers take on the task with the help of real estate agents and their multiple listing service. As a seller, you pay the agent a commission to list and sell your home. The national commission average is 6 percent of the selling price, but some agents charge as little as 3 or 4 percent, and in some parts of the country agents take an incredible 10 percent of the selling price. You may be able to negotiate a lower fee, especially if you are willing to list with the agent exclusively for a specified time (that means the agent won't put your house on the MLS and you can't register the house with other agents). Agents will show your house to prescreened prospective buyers when you're not around, too, which is an added convenience. But you may be determined to try your hand at selling on your own.

FOR SALE BY OWNER

You may be able to save thousands of dollars in commission costs by selling your house on your own. Selling a house by yourself is a lot of work, however. Can you take time away from work or other obligations to do what's necessary, such as preparing house brochures, opening your door to strangers to show them around during working hours and on the weekend, and taking phone calls at all hours?

Start by getting a report called a *comparative market analysis*, which details the sales of similar houses in your area. Since you are selling the house on your own you can't get this analysis from a real estate agent. However, several online resources, such as www.homepages.com, let you search recent home sales in your region, including the real estate sections of your local newspapers. Look for sales of houses similar in size, location, and condition to yours and create your own report. Use it to help you set the price. Many buyers believe that a house being sold by the owner should be less expensive than a home being offered through a realtor. They feel that they should be saving money since the seller isn't paying a hefty commission. In light of that, you may want to consider shaving a bit from the price—but remain consistent with the figures for home sales in your area. Don't sell yourself short!

Advertise the house in local papers and real estate guides, on the Internet, and with the MLS. To list with the MLS, you generally have to pay a flat fee to a service, such as www.brokerdirectmls.com or www.flatfeemlslisting.com, that takes your listing and adds it to the MLS. Take pictures of your house inside and out to post on the Internet, in ads, and on a sell sheet or brochure, which you should make yourself (see page 33).

Safety when showing your home is also a major concern for do-it-yourselfers. Be cautious about whom you allow through your front door. Never show the house alone. Always have at least one other person with you—a spouse, friend, or family member. Let the buyer enter rooms first. Stay by the door in case a quick exit is necessary. Keep your cell phone handy. Get as much information as possible about a prospective buyer before the showing, then confirm the data. For example, get his or her full name, current address, employer's name, and reason for moving. This brief interview process should also deter "Sunday drivers" who may be curious about the property but have no intention of buying.

Fielding offers may be the most challenging aspect of selling your own home. Real estate agents will verify a buyer's financial or preapproval status before showing him or her a property. Ask prospective buyers if they have been preapproved by a lender for an amount in your price range and then ask for a copy of the preapproval documentation. Find out if they are ready to buy now or if they have to sell their home first to get the money together. If they have to sell, you have to decide whether you can wait until that happens.

If you accept an offer, you have to hire a lawyer to handle the paperwork, including looking over the offer and any contingencies and making sure all documents are in order for and at the closing. Don't try to cut corners when it comes to contracts. The contract should spell out what happens to the buyer's deposit money if the deal falls through. This money does not belong to you until the house is sold or the buyer breaks the contract in such a way that it becomes yours by prior agreement. It will be credited to the buyer's funds on closing day and ideally should be held in escrow (often by your attorney) until then.

Ultimately, you have to decide whether all this work is worth it to save the 6 percent agent's commission—especially if you are working every day and can't devote the time necessary to sell a house on your own.

PROPERTY DISCLOSURES

Most states require sellers to supply potential buyers with a property disclosure form. If you are working with an agent, he or she will help you fill out the necessary paperwork. If not, you have to prepare it yourself. Even if a formal disclosure form isn't legally mandatory, you are probably required by law to tell buyers about known problems, often referred to as material facts. If you're not sure about the law in your community, your town or city hall can help you determine what you need to disclose. Here's a look at the information that is typically included in a property disclosure:

☐ Age of the home and any additions, renovations, or replacements (for example, the house is 30 years old and the roof is 5 years old)

☐ Existing problems with any aspect of the house (for instance, an empty oil tank buried in the backyard or dampness in the basement)

☐ Persistent pest problems (rodents, termites, and so on)

☐ The existence of your own or a neighbor's structures such as fences or sheds that extend past the property's boundaries

☐ Whether the house sits on an airport flight path or geologic fault or in a flood zone

☐ For houses built prior to 1978, federal law requires disclosure that the home could contain lead-based paint and details about past testing for lead paint. You must also offer buyers the opportunity to do their own lead paint testing.

☐ In some states, whether your house is known to be haunted or if a violent crime was committed there!

on your own

Create a House Brochure

Whether or not you use an agent to sell your house, you can actively participate in the process by showing off your home to its best advantage with a sell sheet or brochure. Most of the time, the one-page fact sheet a buyer gets from a real estate agency includes a fuzzy black-and-white photo of the outside of the home; a list of basic information about the house, including square footage, number of bedrooms and bathrooms, and details such as wood floors or a tiled kitchen; and the asking price and yearly property taxes. But there is so much more information you can provide in a beautiful way. No one knows your house as intimately as you do. You have this opportunity to describe the special features and unique attributes that make your house a home—why not take it? It's very easy and effective, and since so few people actually take the time to create a brochure, making one will put your house a step above the rest.

How much will it cost? If you plan on taking your brochure to a copy shop, count on spending between three and five cents each for multiple copies of black-and-white pages and between 50 cents and a dollar for each copy of color pages. You could spend around $200 for 50 to 100 copies of your brochure.

What do I need? You really need very few tools—even more reason to do it! Reserve a quiet afternoon for the task.

Digital or conventional camera

Computer

Color printer or access to a color copier

How do I do it?

1. Take several digital or conventional photos of your house, both inside and out. If you don't have a digital camera, ask the photo processor to create a CD from your film so you can load the photos onto your computer.

2. Create a new document in a photo-friendly software program such as SmartDraw Certificate and Flyer Edition or Avanquest's Design and Print, or use Microsoft Word's built-in templates to make a brochure and use the basic photo system that comes with your software package to place pictures into the document.

3. Insert photo files of your home's exterior—front and back—on the first page of the document.

4. Use the templates provided with your software package or keep it simple and center the name of the residence and the address above the photos. For example: Kavovit Residence, 123 Alphabet Lane, Anytown, NY. Place the contact information for your real estate agent—or yourself, if you are selling the house—beneath the photos.

5. Place photos of the two most impressive rooms in your house on page 2. Those might be the kitchen and living room, or the master bedroom and bathroom. If you have extra-special landscaping, your yard might pack the biggest wow. Beneath the photos, list the square footage of the home, the number of rooms (specify the number of bedrooms and bathrooms), and the finishes used in each room. For example, if the

789 SMITH LANE, YOUR TOWN, NJ 12345

LISTING AGENT: Jane Doe (609) 555-5678

LIST PRICE: $525,000

Charming 3-bedroom, 2½ bath expanded Cape Cod located on one of the borough's prettiest tree-lined streets—picturesque in every season—and conveniently located within walking distance to Your Town Elementary and the Smith Lane Park. Owners have recently added new landscaping and updated kitchen appliances.

- Taxes (2005): $7,865

- 1,900 sq. feet

- Lot size: .39 acre

- Large and sunny eat-in kitchen/family room combo with French doors opening onto a brand-new deck with new gas grill connected to main gas line

- Spacious master bedroom and bath including steam shower and Jacuzzi tub

- Cozy formal living room with original brick wood-burning fireplace

- Insulated sunroom with bay windows and vaulted ceilings, perfect for a game room, dining room, or home office.

- Original oak hardwood floors throughout; ceramic tile in kitchen and bathrooms

- Mudroom with large-capacity washer and dryer and plenty of storage

- Watertight unfinished basement with extra refrigerator (perfect for entertaining!)

- Central air and forced-air gas heat

This is a rare gem in a highly desirable neighborhood and won't last long!

kitchen and bathroom have a ceramic tile floor, list that. If there are any special features about the materials used in the house, put them down. For example, if you used Italian marble for your bathroom countertops, make a note of it. If your kitchen countertops are high-end quartz, say so. If you have recently upgraded any appliances that you are offering with the house, make that clear. Don't be shy about advertising the unique features in your home. Don't just say "hardwood floors"—if they're oak, say, "oak hardwood floors, lovingly cared for."

6. Use page 3 to describe the special features or renovations that suggest quality, excellent maintenance, and a desirable lifestyle to the buyer. Buyers like to know that the floors are restored and that the kitchen has been recently renovated. Turn potential drawbacks into advantages and highlight them. Instead of trying to disguise the fact that the third bedroom is tiny, say instead, "Cozy den makes a perfect retreat for reading, working, or simply napping." (Make sure you stage the room to look like a den!)

7. Include a copy of the property survey in the brochure. This important piece of information shows buyers the potential of the entire property— which is very appealing to someone who has construction or renovation on his or her mind.

8. Print, copy, collate, and staple your brochures.

9. Finally, place the brochures in a conspicuous place in your home—the foyer or entryway, dining room table, or kitchen island are all good choices.

OPEN HOUSE SUCCESS

An open house creates excitement and lets a lot of people view the property at once. Even if your neighbors who have no intention of buying come by (and this will happen), they may have friends and friends of friends who are interested in buying a house—and if they like what they see, they will spread the word. Make sure your open house is a success by:

☐ Placing your house brochure in conspicuous locations around the house

☐ Replacing lightbulbs with bulbs of the highest wattage the fixtures will allow and turning on all the lights—bright houses are more appealing than dark ones

☐ Keeping draperies and window coverings open

☐ Placing a bowl of fresh fruit such as apples or lemons and limes on the kitchen island or table

☐ Making sure the bathroom towels are clean (or new), beautifully folded, and stacked or hung

☐ Setting your dining room or kitchen table for a meal with your prettiest china and best linen napkins

☐ Storing accumulated mail out of sight and tossing old newspapers and magazines

☐ Cleaning out the fireplace and stacking new logs; if it's cold outside, build a fire

☐ Turning off the TV and softly playing jazz or classical music

☐ Grinding up a fresh lemon or orange in the garbage disposal or simmering some cinnamon and cloves in a pot of water on the stove

☐ Locking up or securely storing small valuables

☐ Keeping pets securely penned or contained so they don't frighten buyers or escape during a viewing

LET'S MAKE A DEAL

There will come a time—sometimes within just days or weeks of putting your house on the market—when you will receive offers. Your agent will field these offers on your behalf. If you are selling the house yourself, you will have to take the offers and weigh them yourself, and you can certainly ask your attorney to advise you. Because the agent wants to sell your house to make his or her commission, he or she may be eager for you to accept the first proposal that comes along. Don't feel pressured to accept any offer you deem too low. Make a counteroffer or stick to your asking price if you think it was fair. However, if your home has been on the market for 6 weeks or more before you receive the first offer, you should evaluate it carefully. Can you afford to keep your house on the market and wait for a higher offer? If someone offers to buy your house at its asking price, you generally have to accept it—unless, of course, there's a bidding war for your property; then you can choose among the best offers.

Once you accept an offer, get it in writing. An offer is a legal transaction as well as a financial one. All real estate sales contracts include the same basic information. Along with a legal description of the property ("single-family, three bedroom house") and its street address, the offer will include its selling price, financing and inspection contingencies (if applicable), and the specifics of the mortgage regarding the amount, rate, and term and when the application for the mortgage will be made. Other items that show up on a contract include:

- [ ] The amount of the deposit and who holds it

- [ ] The date, location, and time of the closing

- [ ] A list of particular items that are or are not included in the sale of the property

- [ ] The parameters of the home inspection, including when it will be completed

- [ ] Any warranties and what they cover

- [ ] Well water and septic system test results, if applicable or necessary

- [ ] Termite and pest inspections and who will pay for taking care of infestation or damage

- [ ] The date the buyer takes possession of the house

- [ ] The number of days the seller has to respond to the offer with either acceptance or a counteroffer

- [ ] Any provisions for arbitration of disputes

- [ ] The name of the policyholders of the insurance that covers the property until the closing date

- [ ] The property disclosure form

The sale will likely be contingent on an inspection and the buyer's securing financing. If the buyer is preapproved, the transaction will move quickly. If not, you may have to wait a few weeks for the deal to be done. Closings are usually scheduled for a few weeks after that. You must be ready to move out of your house as soon as the deal is completed. Time seems to move faster once a house goes to contract, so it's best to start packing your possessions and arranging for a mover as soon as you can. You'll also want to be prepared to move into your new place as soon as possible, especially if you are buying and selling simultaneously.

———————— ! ————————

Once you've moved, you'll want to start finding ways to increase your new home's value as soon as the last box is unpacked. Doing so might even include making some major changes and renovations. Let's not waste any time!

PART 2

THE
BIG
PICTURE

There are degrees of difficulty to everything in life, and that certainly includes improving your home. With the right tools and information, however, you can accomplish anything you set your mind to, including adding dollars to your home's price tag. Many improvements start with what's behind the walls—the stuff that makes your house hum, like the plumbing; electrical; and heating, ventilating, and air-conditioning (HVAC) systems—not to mention the floors and walls themselves. Part 2 gives you the lowdown on these aspects of your home, what you should pay attention to, and why the pros play such an important role in their installation and upkeep.

I won't try to convince you that dealing with wiring, pipes, and ductwork is the most exciting part of being a home owner. It's not. On the other hand, if providing energy to light rooms, run appliances, and power entertainment systems; pipes to transfer hot and cold running water; and conduits to maintain good air quality don't add comfort and value to a home, I don't know what does. Once you understand and appreciate your home's mechanical systems, you will be able to ask for and get exactly what you want when it comes time to make an improvement—whether you do it yourself or hire a professional—and this kind of satisfaction is one of the great joys of home ownership!

Even if you own an apartment or townhouse, you are ultimately responsible for what's directly behind your walls. Don't pass up the opportunity to learn a little bit about the way your house works from the inside out. Look at it this way: If the big picture is in good shape, you're free to concentrate on the decorating and personal touches, like refreshing your kitchen cabinets or hanging new window treatments.

!

CHAPTER 3

The Inside Story

How many times have you wondered how certain things work, how they are wired, and what literally makes them tick? Perhaps not very often, because when the systems of a house are working well, you hardly notice them. It's only when a circuit breaker blows or a pipe bursts that you think about what's going on behind the scenes. You can't possibly own and live in your home, spend most of your time there, and not understand the basic elements of how you get water, electricity, heat, and air. I am not saying you need to be a rocket scientist and know how to wire your house, but it is vital that you know some basic facts. For plumbing, the basic concepts are how you get running water, produce hot water, and remove waste. For electrical systems, the key things to know are where your service panel is and how the breakers inside it bring power into your home—and how they help protect your family, too. For HVAC systems, your home's breathing unit, you need to understand how air circulates through your house, how it is cooled, and how rooms are heated, whether the system uses air or hot water.

You might think old wiring or bad plumbing is reason enough to pass up or move out of a house or condo in a great location. Don't be deterred. You can hire professionals to change or update the systems. While you can do some simple fixes yourself, many of the jobs having to do with the infrastructure of your home are best left to the professionals. Amateurs tinkering with wires and pipes can cause real disasters, and your home-owner's insurance policy may not cover damage done by do-it-yourself plumbers and electricians. Tackling such projects yourself just isn't worth the risk, especially since in the long run you probably won't save any money.

go to the pros

HIRE A MECHANICAL SPECIALIST

I have built and renovated a lot of houses and commercial spaces, so I know how important it is to find the right people to help you get jobs done. How do you do it? First, get rid of any fears you might have about talking to a plumber, electrician, or HVAC specialist. The only way to learn is to dive right in. I have been dealing with skeptics my whole life—including those who carry pipe wrenches and wire cutters in their toolboxes! Don't let them intimidate you. You likely have good instincts—use them when you're hiring tradespeople. Here are a few things I've learned after many years on the job.

Who are these people?

Plumbers install and repair pipes, fixtures (faucets, sinks, bathtubs), and related equipment for water distribution and wastewater removal.

Electricians assemble, install, repair, maintain, connect, and test wiring and electrical fixtures.

HVAC specialists install and repair home heating, ventilating, and cooling systems using many skills, including both plumbing and electric.

Where do I find them?

There's no secret to this—recommendations are your best resource, and word of mouth is a professional's best advertising tool. If you are new in town and don't know anyone to ask for a name or two, check online for neighborhood or block association home improvement bulletin boards. They are one of the many advantages of the networked society. You will be surprised at how many good neighbors use these sites to recommend contractors and tradespeople who do good work and warn about others who do poor work. If all else fails, you know the drill: Check the yellow pages of your telephone directory. Here are some tips that will help you if you're working without a recommendation:

What kind of training and certification do they need?

All professional tradespeople should be licensed by the state they work in; specific qualifications vary by region. The bottom line is that you have to hire someone with an up-to-date license or their mistakes (if they make any) won't be covered by their insurance or yours. His or her license number should be printed on the business card and even on the side of the truck or van. Call your state's contractor licensing board to verify the contractor's credentials and confirm that the license is valid. Every professional you hire must also have an active insurance policy. Ask to see the policy or, better yet, request a copy of the policy with the insurer's name on it. Then call the company to make sure the policy is legit. I have checked on tradespeople's insurance policies only to find out that their insurance had lapsed. Don't overlook this important step!
Call your local Department of Consumer Affairs and Better Business Bureau branch to find out if there are any unresolved complaints on files against the specialist. If serious problems are pending, steer clear. Ask the contractor for references—and call them! Visit the jobs they've done. Ask previous customers if they like the work that was done, if problems were resolved quickly, and if they would use the person or company again.

The license is in order—now what? Which guy is right for my job?

Get at least three detailed, written estimates. Request that the estimate cover the entire scope of the work, including the removal and disposal of old fixtures (tubs, sinks), materials (old ductwork, wiring), and debris. You don't want to be stuck doing trash duty when the work is done!

This is also your chance to meet the candidates face-to-face. It's so important to pay attention to body language. These people perform a service that you pay for. Judge them as you would a potential employee—that's what they are. Do they look you in the eye, answer your questions directly, and treat you with respect? I've been in the building business for a long time, and I still come across men who don't like working for a woman. My easy solution: I don't hire them. You don't have to either. You should expect nothing less than professional, courteous service when you're writing the checks.

When you've gotten three or more bids, compare them. Are they similar? If the bids are within 10 to 15 percent of each other, the estimates are most likely a fair reflection of the going rate for work in your area. Who has the best references? Which one showed up on time and got back to you promptly with a bid? Who had a neat presentation and good personal hygiene? I'm not kidding—these things say a lot about the level of workmanship you will get. If someone's a messy dresser or has a cluttered truck, that may carry over to the work site (your house!).

If one of the bids is much lower than the other two (30 percent or more), it's probably too good to be true and, in my experience, additional costs will pile up once the job has begun. The company or tradesperson is enticing you with a low bid to get your business and may try to recoup the money in additional, allegedly unforeseen labor or material costs. If one bid is much higher, it might be a sign that the tradesperson is in financial trouble and needs cash or is trying to take advantage of you.

I have accepted one of the bids. What's next?

The specialist should give you a contract, which your lawyer can review (although it's not necessary). The contract should include:

Estimated start and completion dates

General conditions of the job. (they should have been included in the estimate): These are direct costs associated with the job, such as rubbish removal, supervision, and insurance for temporary protection against liability.

Cost estimate

Payment schedule. Limit deposits and up-front payments to material costs only. A reputable established plumber, electrician, or HVAC pro generally will not ask for a deposit on labor. Back off if they do; it's a bad sign. Keep payments for labor tied to work completed and keep a schedule of completed work. Ask for receipts before paying for additional materials.

Materials to be used for the project. The brand name and model number of specific fixtures and installed equipment should be specified. You don't want to pay for one brand of air conditioner and get another!

Overhead and profit. Not every professional will give you this figure, so don't panic if it isn't included. However, according to one trade association, most plumbing, electrical, and HVAC contractors say that the minimum markup to keep them in business is 50 percent of direct job costs, which translates into a 33 percent gross profit.

They've started working. Should I do anything?

While you may not be able to look over a worker's shoulder every minute he or she is in your house, you do need to supervise them. Be home when they are working if you can or arrange for someone else to be there. Make sure the contractor knows how to contact you at home and at work, in case a problem arises. If you aren't happy with the work once it's done or you do not feel that the terms of the contract have been fulfilled, you can withhold the final payment until you are satisfied with the job.

THE ELECTRIC HOUSE

A house has to be wired for light, sound, work, and play. We take outlets and switches for granted because we are so used to simply flipping a switch or pushing a button to watch a movie, play a game, listen to music, or read a book. Upgrading and adding to the wiring in your house for maximum capacity is an excellent way to expand the power of your home and what you can do in it.

Before you even consider having electrical work done, find the electrical service panel, learn how the circuit breakers or fuses inside the panel work, and do a quick inspection of the visible electrical components in your house. Label each circuit breaker or fuse by writing the room or rooms it controls on a piece of white tape placed next to the breaker switch. Why? It's essential that you familiarize yourself with how to operate the master power supply, especially if you want to tackle simple tasks like replacing a light fixture and installing dimmers on light switches.

I am always surprised by how many people have no idea how to shut the power off in their house—or turn it back on when a circuit overloads and the power shuts off. In a house, the service panel usually is located in the basement or utility room; in a condo or apartment, it's often found in the kitchen or entryway.

To turn the power off at the service panel, stand on a dry, nonconductive "grounding" surface such as a rubber mat. Standing in even a small puddle of water can conduct electricity through your body. Use one hand to flip the breaker switch or unscrew the fuse. Keep your other hand behind you or in your pocket so you will not be tempted to touch something that could conduct electricity.

PERFORM AN ELECTRIC INSPECTION

A visual inspection helps you identify what an electrician needs to do in your house—it gives you a starting point for repairs and improvements. So grab a pencil and paper and take a tour of your home, noting the condition of the following electrical components:

Service panel door. It should be accessible from the front, open easily, and close securely. The panel itself should be sealed to prevent contact with live parts of the wiring system. If any wiring is exposed or if the box is rusty or doesn't close properly, have a pro replace it.

Switches, outlets, and visible junction boxes. A junction box is a metal box used to enclose the meeting (junction) of electrical circuits, wires, and cables. Check to make sure they, as well as switches and outlets, are in working order and covered to protect you from electric shock. Buy and install plate covers for outlets that are missing them. A licensed electrician must replace any junction box that is "open," or uncovered, with one that has a secure front cover (open junction boxes are often found in utility rooms, basements, and attics).

Frayed or bare wires. If you see any wires that have damaged or missing plastic coating, which serves as insulation, have them replaced immediately. Do not touch an exposed wire; call a licensed electrician to repair or replace it. Also, make sure that all wires are securely bundled together and not hanging loose.

Bathrooms and kitchen. Do you have enough outlets around your countertops? Check for ground-fault circuit interrupter wall outlets (the outlets that have one slot that is bigger than the other). Bathrooms and kitchens must include at least one of these. They should also have at least one permanently installed ceiling- or wall-mounted light fixture.

Other rooms. Do bedrooms, family rooms, and entryways have enough outlets and overhead light fixtures? If not, consider having wires run for additional outlets and permanent fixtures. A good rule of thumb is that there should be at least two outlets per 10-foot length of wall.

Exterior. What about outdoor outlets? Are they in working order? Replace old exterior outlets that show signs of rust or wear or are inoperable.

ELECTRICAL UPGRADE IDEAS

There are many ways you can work with a licensed electrician (see page 44) to improve the flow of energy in your house. Here are some valuable upgrade ideas:

Upgrade the service

If you live in an older home with a service panel that uses fuses, update to a system with circuit breakers. The main advantage of toggle-switch circuit breakers over fuses is that they don't have to be replaced every time the circuit is blown, as fuses do.

If your vintage pad is wired with only 120-volt service, switch to today's standard dual system, which brings the household total up to 240 volts. If only two wires enter your house from the utility pole instead of the standard three wires, you probably only have 120-volt capacity. A 240-volt system is essential if you plan to use modern appliances, powerful ovens, and energy-efficient air-conditioning and heating units. Even the powerful new vacuum cleaners can blow a 120-volt circuit. Running many appliances on an undersize system will tax its limits and could be a fire hazard.

How long does it take? One or 2 days, depending on the size and complexity of your existing system

How much will it cost? Prices vary by region, so it could run $750 to $1,500 or much more, depending on where you live.

What happens? An electrician will run a new and larger service cable to your service panel from your utility company's distribution line, install a new service panel with toggle-style circuit breakers, and then hook up the old circuits to the new panel.

Install ground-fault circuit interrupters

According to the National Electrical Code, which most communities have adopted as part of their building code, ground-fault circuit interrupters (GFCIs) must be installed in areas near water, such as bathrooms, kitchens, garages, utility rooms, unfinished basements, and outdoor locations. GFCIs protect you from hazardous ground faults by automatically turning off the electricity to the unit when a fault is detected. When a GFCI senses that electrical current in a circuit is leaking to ground, it will trip the circuit, interrupting the power in time to prevent serious injury from electrical shock. GFCIs protect you in case you drop a blow dryer into a sink full of water or if the cord of a small kitchen appliance slides into a sink full of wet dishes. If you have such units already installed in your home, don't underestimate their value for your own and your family's protection.

How long does it take? One or 2 days, depending on the size and complexity of your existing system

How much will it cost? It can cost $50 to $150 per outlet for professional installation or about $10 to $20 per adaptor (see below). Prices vary by region.

What happens? An electrician will remove the existing outlet boxes, replace them with GFCI boxes, and replace the outlet covers. You don't necessarily have to have an electrician hardwire GFCI units into the required areas (although at some point it is a good idea to do so). Instead, you can purchase GFCI adaptors at home improvement stores. Remove the cover plate of the existing outlet and plug the GFCI adaptor directly into your receptacle.

Replace wiring that has deteriorating insulation

This common problem occurs when wiring has been exposed to extremes of hot and cold, like in an attic. Mice can also gnaw at wire insulation if it's in the way of a hole they're determined to get through. An exposed wire can easily spark and cause a fire. Not long ago, my friend Randy was trying to plug a mouse hole with steel wool. He did not see that a mouse had exposed a wire on the other side of the opening by gnawing away the insulating coating. Sparks flew when he stuffed the steel wool into the hole and it contacted the wire. Luckily, Randy was okay, but it could have injured him or started a fire. Exposed wires are a real danger!

How long does it take? Half a day to 5 days, depending on the size and complexity of the problem

How much will it cost? Prices vary by region, but probably $200 to $2,000, depending on the size and complexity of the problem

What happens? The electrician removes the existing wall and attic thermal insulation, replaces the old wiring, and then puts in new thermal insulation. Ask your electrician if he or she recommends using wire covered with a metal hose (or conduit) in weather- and rodent-exposed areas like attics or basements.

Replace light fixture boxes

Hardwired light fixtures are rated to a particular wattage for safety. Still, we sometimes use higher-wattage bulbs (by placing, for example, a 100-watt bulb in a fixture and junction box that are rated for a 60-watt bulb), either because we never knew or have forgotten what the capacity is. This can cause a fuse to blow and, potentially, a fire. If you want to replace light fixtures around your house, old junction boxes with deteriorating wiring must be replaced with new boxes that can handle higher-wattage bulbs.

How long does it take? One or 2 days

How much will it cost? Prices vary by region, but $200 to $500 to replace five to eight fixture boxes

What happens? The electrician removes all the old fixture boxes and wiring and replaces them with components that can handle higher wattage. Ask the electrician to pay special attention to kitchen fixture outlets. These tend to be in the worst condition because kitchen lights are often left on constantly or are turned on and off frequently. Frequent use equals wear and tear.

Replace older, two-prong receptacles
with grounded or three-prong receptacles

Old two-prong outlets that don't have a wider "grounding" slot are not functional for modern life. Modern lamps and many small appliances have either two-prong plugs on which one blade is wider than the other or three-prong plugs that include a ground prong. These plugs will not fit into old outlets, so you'll need to upgrade.

How long does it take? One or 2 days

How much will it cost? Prices vary by region, but $50 to $200 per outlet

What happens? The electrician removes the old outlets and installs three-prong outlets.

comfort zone

ADD A DATA CENTER

Even if you live in a 19th-century bungalow or a 1950s modern ranch house, you have a 21st-century lifestyle—and most likely have one or more telephones, at least one computer with a high-speed DSL telephone-line connection, multiple television sets with cable or satellite hookups, and possibly a high-end sound system. Why not consider installing a data center? A data center is a metal cabinet approximately the size of your electrical service panel that can accommodate data jacks for all your communication equipment. This box becomes the central location where all cable, Internet, and phone service enters your house.

Who does it? *An electrician who specializes in data wiring*

How long does it take?

From 1 day to a week

How much will it cost? *This is a pricey system to retrofit, making it optional for many home owners. Prices start at $2,500 and vary by region.*

What happens? *The electrician installs a data box in an easily accessible closet or near the electrical service panel. This involves making a hole in the wall and then patching it up. From that point, all cables are distributed to individual rooms in a plan that electricians call structured wiring. He or she then installs data outlets in the rooms. The outlets for a structured wiring network usually have four jacks, two for cable and one each for phone and data transmission.*

PLUMB CRAZY!

Many home owners are especially timid about plumbing because it seems so complex and out of reach. But, given what plumbing actually does for us—carry clean water into and wastewater out of our homes—it's fairly basic and efficient.

If you are considering redoing your bathroom or kitchen, plumbing is a central aspect of those jobs. If you want to change the location of a sink or toilet, or add a large shower, a plumber will have to relocate existing fixtures. Before you install that at-home spa or restaurant stove, though, you have to identify the main water shutoff source in your house. It is usually near where the first water pipe comes in from the street, often in the basement. If you are currently buying the house, ask the previous owner or the house inspector to show you where it is and how to operate it. There may be times when you need to shut off the water coming into your house. You also need to know the locations of all the local

barbara's best bet

PIPE HYPE

What you select for pipe material depends on what you are using it for. Basically it comes down to a choice between metal and plastic—and it's likely that you will find both already in your house. When selecting replacement piping, copper is the material of choice for supply-line (water) plumbing since it is long lasting and durable. Most new homes are built with copper pipes. Another option for piping material is plastic tubing called CPVC.

CPVC pipes are joined with glue, whereas copper pipes are heated and joined together with solder. Finally, you can also choose PVC water pipe. It's also less expensive than copper and, when joined with a solvent, it creates a very tight seal. Cast iron is the pipe of choice for sewage lines in your home, although some plumbers use PVC piping in this application. Cast iron is much quieter and longer lasting than its plastic counterpart.

shutoff valves for the pipes under sinks and near toilets and the washing machine. You will eventually need to shut one off to make minor repairs to or replace fixtures or faucets, so there's no time like the present to familiarize yourself with the basics.

PLUMBING UPGRADE IDEAS

Here are some whole-house plumbing upgrades you should be aware of before tackling plumbing changes in specific rooms:

Put the Pressure On

Good water pressure throughout your home is a necessity! It won't matter how fancy your kitchen sink or whirlpool bathtub is if the water's not pressurized enough or coming through a pipe of the proper size. Check the water pressure at all fixtures in

comfort zone

GET YOURSELF IN HOT WATER

When you turn on the hot water in your shower, bathtub, or kitchen sink, you always have to wait a bit for the hot water to actually start coming through. A hot-water recirculator is the secret to instantly getting hot water. In the past, they could only be built into new houses, but now you can retrofit them into existing plumbing systems. A family of four can waste 16,000 gallons a year just waiting for hot water to arrive at the faucet! A hot-water recirculator lets you have it when you want it.

How long does it take? *About half a day*

How much will it cost? *Between $250 and $500 for the system, plus another $500 and up for labor*

What happens? *A plumber installs an instant hot-water kit, which often includes a timer-operated pump and a bypass valve. Recirculating systems don't require any new pipes. The pump mounts on the existing hot-water pipe that exits the water heater. The plumber then installs a bypass valve under the sink that is farthest from the water heater and is plumbed to connect the hot- and cold-water supply pipes. The timer can be set to activate the pump for morning showers or evening baths—or any interval of your choice.*

your house. Turn on all the faucets (including tubs, showers, and garden hoses) at once; is the pressure good? Flush the toilet while the shower is on; is water pressure maintained or does it go way down? If it goes down, you might want to have a professional take a look.

How long does it take? A couple of hours if valves need to be opened, up to a week if a buried water line must be dug up

How much will it cost? The price varies widely. It can cost anywhere from $200 to $1,000 or much more, depending on the complexity of the problem. For example, the water company may open the valves at the meter for no charge. A plumber may charge $100 to examine and open valves, but other repairs, especially those that require digging, can cost much more.

What happens? The plumber will examine the valves on either side of the water meter. If it's an outdoor meter in an underground pit, he or she will use a special socket wrench to open the meter box cover to make sure the valves are fully open. If all of the valves are fully open at the same time and the water pressure is still low, there could be a restriction in the line in the house, or the buried portion of the water line leading to your home from the street could be crushed or blocked. First the plumber will break open the water line at the water meter to check the water volume and pressure. If it's good there, then the problem is somewhere between that point and your home. Get out the shovels! The plumber will dig out the line, find the obstruction, fix it, and fill in the trench.

Prevent Sewage from Flooding Your Basement!

When sewage backs up into your basement, it creates a disgusting mess (to say the least!) that can be expensive to clean up and harmful to your health. Basement flooding due to sewer backup can happen during heavy rainstorms, but you can make adjustments in your plumbing to keep this from happening.

How long does it take? About a day

How much will it cost? Pumps with installation can cost anywhere from $1,500 for a basic sump pump and $2,500 for a sump pump with valves to $4,500 or more for a sump pump and ejector valve.

What happens? A plumber installs a basic sump pump to remove drain water from around the basement wall and discharge it to the surface of the ground or into a ditch or a storm sewer, depending on the surface grading around the house. If a sump pump isn't good enough on its own, the plumber will install a check valve and a shutoff valve for additional protection. This is what I recommend. The valves isolate the house plumbing from the public sewer in the street. The check valve includes a flapper that shuts when the water level in the public sewer is high enough to flow back into the house. The shutoff valve can be manually closed as an added measure. A combination sump pump and ejector pump is the ultimate in protection. The ejector pump transfers sewage into the public sewer whether it is flooded or not.

HEAT UP AND COOL DOWN

A good heating and cooling system is essential to your comfort and health. It seems to me that every winter gets a bit colder and the summers get a little hotter—maybe it's global warming, maybe it's a weather cycle, or perhaps it's a combination of both. One thing I do know for sure is that spending a night huddled under blankets because the heat's not functioning or trying to get anything done in a hot house on a steamy day is a miserable and uncomfortable feeling.

go to the pros

GET HELP UNDERSTANDING YOUR HEATING AND COOLING SYSTEMS

Most homes are heated by hot air, water, or steam that is circulated throughout the house from a central furnace. Old systems rely on gravity to move warm air or water through the system to heat your house. Newer systems use blowers or circulating pumps to move warm air through a system of radiators. The furnace for any of these systems can be powered by natural gas, propane gas, oil, or electricity.

Since systems are so varied, there just is not enough space in this book to go through them all and describe the myriad major repairs that might be required. I recommend that you ask an HVAC professional to assess yours and teach you

comfort zone

RADIANT FLOORS

Radiant heat floor systems are a modern, cozy heat-delivery system. Electric coils that are well distributed just under the flooring surface throughout the room provide the heat. Such systems make cool tile and stone floors warm underfoot in the winter. Radiant heat floors are a great way to heat additions or rooms that are not attached to the existing heat system, like an enclosed sunporch. Each area or room usually has a dial control that lets you decide whether to heat it and how warm you want to make it. Many systems can be set to turn on automatically to warm the room before you get up and then shut off at a certain time in the evening. Heaven!

Who does it? *An HVAC specialist. Some simple systems can be installed by a flooring contractor. If you hire a flooring pro, an electrician should make the necessary connections. An HVAC specialist can install and hook up the system.*

How long does it take? *About 1 day per room*

How much will it cost? *From $2,000 to $5,000, and possibly more, per room, depending on the type of system you're installing and the size of the room; this does not include the flooring that will eventually be placed on top of the system*

What happens? *The HVAC specialist will install whatever system you choose, usually a system of coils, and hook it up to a control dial on the wall of the room where the system is located. Once it is in place, a flooring contractor will place a floor over it. Manufacturers are always coming up with new ways to make radiant heating easier to install, since it is gaining in popularity. One new radiant floor product acts a bit like an electric blanket and can be installed beneath tile, stone, hardwood laminates, and even carpet. It's a thin mesh with small electrical coils snaked across it—you roll it out, hook it up, and then place the new flooring on top. A flooring contractor can install it fairly easily, and the labor costs should be low. A licensed electrician should make the appropriate electrical connections.*

seasonal and year-round maintenance and troubleshooting basics. Determine what you can do yourself before the heating or cooling season sets in to reduce the risk of being without heat or cool air when you really need it. Poorly functioning, inefficient heating systems don't perform the way you want them to and end up costing you an arm and a leg to boot, so it really pays to make sure you have the most efficient systems and know how to maintain them properly.

$ barbara's best bet

CLEAN AIR IS PRICELESS

Whatever heating system you have should be maintained on a regular basis to ensure that clean air is pumped through your home. If your system uses disposable filters, change them monthly during the heating season. For a system with a permanent filter, put on a pair of rubber work gloves and pull out the filter pad to clean it with mild soap and water. Rinse it thoroughly and replace. Remove registers in rooms and vacuum the openings at the beginning of and a minimum of twice a month during the heating season, and dust off the register itself. Breathe deeply!

Who does it?
An HVAC specialist

How long does it take?
Evaluating your system and taking you through all the maintenance and trouble-shooting steps should take no more than 2 to 3 hours. If a serious problem is uncovered, it can take from half a day to 2 to 3 days to fix it, depending on what's involved.

How much will it cost?
If a review of the system and its care and a minor adjustment or replacement part is all that's required, expect to pay at least $50 to $100 per hour for the specialist's time, plus materials. Major repairs, replacements, and upgrades to heating systems can start at $1,500 and go up from there, reaching several thousand dollars for entirely new systems. A seasonal start-up service call, in which the HVAC pro does a quick check of your system and recommends further maintenance if necessary, can be done in the fall and should cost only about $75.

What happens?

During a standard system review, the HVAC pro will walk you through the heating and cooling systems. On the heating end, he or she will show you how to clean filters, drain the boiler, reignite the pilot light, and replace small parts. For cooling, he or she can show you how to change and clean filters and perform basic maintenance that is unique to your system.

go to the pros

ADD CENTRAL AIR

Air-conditioning cools the house by removing excess heat and reducing humidity. That increases your comfort. AC systems also reduce mold and mildew growth and minimize seasonal swelling and shrinking of wood items, such as floors, doors (which often stick when it's humid), and cabinetry. The ability to control the temperature in your home all year long is such an advantage. It is so much more enjoyable to spend time in a room that's comfortable and cool during hot weather. After having just gone through a really hot summer in New York, I am so grateful that I have a good cooling system at home.

How long does it take?

Two or 3 days to install a simple system in a small house or condo, and up to a week for a very complicated system in a large house

How much will it cost?

Expect to pay from a few to several thousand dollars—in many cases upward of $10,000—to retrofit a whole-house system, depending on how the pro has to duct the system.

Who does it?

An HVAC specialist

What happens?

An HVAC pro will determine what kind of system you need based on how much space you have to install and route the interior equipment, which includes a lot of ductwork. There are three different kinds of central air-conditioning units: low or medium velocity, high velocity, and ductless mini-split. All of them have the same basic interior and exterior components:

Compressor

Expansion valve or metering device

Evaporator coil

Blower or air handler

A low- or medium-velocity system is the most common. A large fan blows air across an evaporator coil to chill and dry the air. That air travels through insulated ductwork and is distributed to each room through smaller flexible ducts. Often installers place the blower in an attic or basement, so a home built on a slab or one with a very small attic crawl space may not be able to accommodate this type of system. High-velocity systems are similar to conventional low or medium ones, but their equipment is substantially smaller, making them appropriate for homes that don't have adequate attic or basement space. Small, flexible tubular ducts are snaked through ceiling joists, much as electrical conduits are. The blower is small enough to fit into a pint-size crawl space. Small is beautiful, but it's also expensive. These systems cost more than conventional units to buy and install, but over the long term they cost less to operate and dehumidify better than their bigger counterparts. A ductless mini-split system is the most expensive of the three, but it's also the easiest to retrofit into an existing home. There are no ducts to leak cool air or absorb heat in hot attics. And you can cool by room, which you cannot do with a traditional central air-conditioning system. You install them in the rooms that really need it, such as bedrooms. The system has three main components: an outdoor unit, an indoor mounted evaporator unit, and a wireless remote controller. The outdoor and indoor units are connected via small refrigerant lines that run through a 3-inch opening in the wall or ceiling. They're perfect for new additions, retrofits, finished basements, and sunrooms in addition to the other existing rooms of the house. With a ductless mini-split you can cool only the space being used, as opposed to central systems that maintain a single temperature throughout the entire house.

Don't you feel cooler because of the knowledge you now have? The operating systems of your house are the silent workhorses that make living in your home easier. Use the basics I've provided here to get the ball rolling and learn as much as you can about the specific systems in your house. Take the time to read manuals and consult with professionals. Don't be afraid to ask questions when a contractor, plumber, or electrician comes to do work. Observe them. Show them that you are curious and want to learn. Most will be flattered and happy to share valuable information (as long as you don't get in their way or inhibit them from doing their jobs!). Next, we will talk about the big-picture elements you can more easily see and feel: windows, doors, walls, and floors. They are the foundation for great style and comfort!

!

CHAPTER 4

Finishes and Function

My windows, doors, floors, and walls say a lot about my home, and they will in yours, too. These features are a significant aspect of living comfortably in your space for years to come. They are the first things you and others see upon entering your home. These structural accents can make your home warm and inviting. Having the right finishes is also extremely important when reselling your home. The finishes in the first house I bought were really modest. I looked at it as a perfect opportunity to rent the house because I did not care about anything getting damaged. But I also thought of them as part of a perfect opportunity for the future, because I knew I could improve them for resale. Buy low, sell high!

I love choosing finishes, too. When I built the house that I live in today, I spent a lot of time researching finishes and applying samples to a board to see how they would complement one another. The floors, walls, windows, and doors became the backdrop for my personal design style.

Great finishes like wooden floors or solid paneled doors with beautiful hardware make a statement—they ooze quality and workmanship, which say *high value*. That's just one reason they are so important. Each also has a very real and important function. Floors are walked on, walls and ceilings create defined spaces, windows let in air and light, and doors help keep us safe and give us privacy. They do a lot, and that's reason enough to celebrate your home's finishes. The good news is that such items can be fairly easily upgraded and replaced as money allows. Great finishes have a positive, long-term effect on the value of your house. Quality details are timeless—and that's a wise investment.

FLOOR IT

There are so many options available in floors nowadays that you'll definitely be able to find something you like that's within your budget. What's your style? Do you want something warm and cozy or dramatic and contemporary? No matter what you prefer, there is something out there for you. Materials come in a seemingly endless variety of colors, finishes, and textures: tile, stone, carpeting, man-made, and, of course, classic wood. And isn't a floor one of the first things you notice when you enter a house? After all, you're standing on it! It's part of the lasting foundation of a good home. The floors set the stage for the furniture you decide to place on them. Your home can go from rustic to modern to traditional and more just by changing the wood and/or finish on the floor. Whatever you spend on good-quality flooring adds two or three times what you paid for it in value to your home. So, for example, if you spend $5,000 on a wood floor, expect that to add from $10,000 to $15,000 or even more to the value of your house.

THE NATURAL BEAUTY OF WOOD

The queen of floors, in my opinion, is tongue-and-groove solid hardwood. It's durable, kid- and pet-friendly, comfortable underfoot, and easy to maintain—not to mention absolutely beautiful. I have always been partial to it. It is warm, earthy, and elegant and looks good in every style of house, from postmodern to midcentury to traditional. I've installed it everywhere, including the kitchen and even a couple of powder rooms—it looks fantastic and wears well. Natural hardwood is the most versatile flooring around—any style of furniture, rug, or drapery looks good against it. And since there are so many options in wood species, plank width, and finish, you can find a style that suits your taste. Plus, wood floors will last throughout the lifetime of a house—and sometimes even longer. Reclaimers take wood floors from deteriorated buildings and rework them so they can be installed again in a new location. Hardwood floors also happen to be the most desirable type of flooring when it comes to property value: Houses with wood flooring sell faster and for higher prices than houses without wood floors. That's money in your pocket!

go to the pros

REFINISH YOUR FLOORS

If you own an older home with hardwood floors, consider yourself lucky! Check out the condition of the floors. If they look scratched and worn, don't worry—refinishing can bring most hardwoods back to their original beauty. Replacing an existing hardwood floor with a new one is much more expensive than restoring the one you have. If I see a house with worn wooden floors, I get excited because I know I can breathe new life into them. My first house, for example, had beautiful hardwood throughout, and refinishing made them look newly installed. A wood floor can be refinished and stained many times over, extending its lifespan and value far beyond those of carpeting and laminates.

Who does it?
A flooring professional who has had at least 5 years of experience in restoring wood floors

How long does it take?
It will take 2 or 3 days to sand, repair, stain, and apply two coats of water-based polyurethane to the floor; the same procedure done using an oil-based finish will take 3 days. If you are going to refinish the floors in your house, do them all at the same time if you can. Considering the time and trouble it takes to do it, it's worth it to get it over with.

How much will it cost?

Average labor costs are about $2 to $2.75 per square foot, so for a 500-square-foot room, it will cost about $1,375. Prices vary by region.

What happens?

Before the refinishers arrive to start the work, clear the room of furniture and draperies. They should supply plastic sheeting to seal the room off and protect adjacent areas from dust—sanding is a messy job even if the refinisher has a dust containment bag attached to his or her sander. At any rate, expect the refinishers to first use an upright drum sander for the large expanses of the room and then a disc edger to get close to baseboards and down narrow hallways. Next they will fill in gouges with wood putty and then apply two or three coats of a protective finish such as polyurethane or tung oil.

---

go to the pros

INSTALL A HARDWOOD FLOOR

If you don't have wood floors and would like to add them, go for it! You will be so happy with the results. Have fun selecting from the gorgeous woods that are available. There are so many options in design, wood species, and color. You can choose light, narrow strips of golden oak, standard 2-inch strips of caramel-colored maple, or 5-inch-wide planks of deep cherry or mahogany in sleek or countrified finishes. You can even install wood reclaimed from a barn or old building for a rustic look that enhances even modern decor. At a dinner party in a Los Angeles home not long ago, I could not stop staring at the owner's beautiful floors. It turned out that they were taken from a 300-year-old barn in Mexico!

Who does it?

A flooring expert with at least 5 years of experience in installing hardwood floors

How long does it take?

It depends on whether you choose prefinished or unfinished flooring. A prefinished floor is more expensive than an unfinished one, but as soon as it's down, you can start using it. A 500-square-foot room can be covered in a day. An unfinished floor has to be sanded, stained, and coated with a protective finish, so the same size room will take 2 or 3 days to complete.

How much will it cost?

Expect installation labor to cost from a minimum of $2.75 to more than $6 per square foot, not including the cost per square foot of the wood. Make sure labor estimates include the removal and replacement of baseboards. Add that to the cost of the flooring itself, which can range from $5 or $6 a square foot for unfinished oak to $12 to $15 for prefinished maple planks to well over $30 per square foot for exotic prefinished mahogany. Antique pine and maple boards that have been removed from one location and planed into planks for reuse can run around $20 or more per square foot. To install a prefinished maple floor in a 500-square-foot room could cost $6,500 to $7,000. Shop around—wood flooring prices are set by supply and demand. Liquidators, who deal in large quantities, may sell your favorite flooring for a lot less than the general prices quoted here. Another hint: January through March are good months to find great deals on wood flooring.

What happens?

Before the installer comes, clear the room of furniture, artwork, and draperies. If you are replacing carpeting with wood, you'll have to pay the installer extra to remove the carpet or do it yourself. A sharp utility knife, some sturdy leather work gloves, a hammer for pulling up nails, and lots of energy are all that's required. Give it a try: Cut sections of rug with the knife starting at the center of the room and working toward the walls, where it is tacked into place on narrow wooden strips. Remove the tack strips by prying them up with the claw end of a hammer.

If the installer is putting the hardwood on top of plywood, he or she will remove the baseboards and number them, place underlayment (a special kind of material called resin paper; it forms a vapor barrier) on the floor, and then nail and glue the planks in place. After that, he or she will replace the baseboards. If it's a prefinished floor, you can put the furniture back in the room. If it's unfinished, the installer will come back the next day to stain and coat the floor.

By the way, I do not recommend installing hardwood directly over concrete because of dampness concerns. The labor involved in building up a concrete floor with a framing system also adds to the cost.

MAGICAL STONE

Although I love wood floors, I see the value in other flooring materials, too. Stone in particular really appeals to me. I especially love it when it's laid next to or even as part of a wood floor, such as a row of slate tiles edging wide, dark oak plank flooring or a field of rich, red granite surrounded by a mahogany border. I have a pale, muted, creamy limestone entryway that leads the way to my living room, which is covered in darkly stained 5-inch-wide planks. The stone tiles are rectangular and rounded (called *pillowed*) and set in a staggered pattern, so there's a lot of movement and texture going on. It is gorgeous and makes the room feel luxurious. Stones such as marble, granite, limestone, and slate are durable, beautiful, textural, and not that difficult to care for. They last forever—and with the right care get even more beautiful over time.

go to the pros

INSTALL A STONE FLOOR

Stone is a natural product delivered courtesy of Mother Earth and a lot of heavy mining equipment; its irregularities are part of its enduring charm. Stone is also heavy and hard—two good reasons that I recommend you hire a professional to lay a stone floor. Do-it-yourselfers would need to be extremely adept at working with a wet saw and carrying heavy materials from a staging area to the installation site. Stone is a premium product better left to an expert who has experience and a feel for working with the material.

Who does it?

A mason who specializes in the cutting and laying of stone. As always, ask for references and, if possible, visit homes where similar work was done so you can inspect it firsthand. It's time well spent: Material and labor costs are high, so you'll want your investment to result in a gorgeous end product.

How long does it take?

Laying a 200-square-foot entryway or bathroom can take 2 to 3 days.

How much will it cost?

Labor can cost anywhere from $5 to $12 per square foot, or much more depending on where you live and the intricacy of the job. When getting quotes, be sure to ask the installer to include the removal and replacement of baseboards. Inlaid wood or combining stones with wood increases the installation costs. Natural stone is usually cut into square-foot tiles, which start at about $3 to $6 for inexpensive slate. Limestone and marble run from $8 to $22 and granite from $10 to $25 per square foot, or much more depending on where you buy it. That means a 200-square-foot area could cost anywhere from $2,000 to $5,600 to install, though you can spend over $100 a square foot for exotic stones or unusual shapes.

What happens?

The installer first removes the baseboards and ensures that the subfloor is sturdy and level. If it is not, he or she may do a "mud job," which is when mortar is prepared from a mixture of portland cement and sand and poured over a membrane of sheathing paper, felt, or polyethylene film that separates the mortar bed from the existing floor. Metal lath sheets are used to enforce the mortar bed. A mud job results in a seamless and very strong foundation for your ceramic or stone tiles. However, it builds up the height of the floor (the mortar bed is 1 inch or more thick, plus a ¼-inch bonding coat of thinset self-leveling mortar or mastic and ⅜ inch for the ceramic or stone tile), so consider that when planning. The installer may also prepare the floor by screwing in cement board and skim coating it with thinset. He or she will cut the stone so it fits around and into odd corners. The next day the installer will come back to grout and polish the floor and replace the baseboards.

COZY CARPETING

Carpeting is another viable flooring option, especially on stairs (where it softens the clatter of feet, both big and little) and in children's bedrooms and playrooms. If you have hardwood floors in bedrooms but like the idea of soft carpeting, think about having a carpet shop cut broadloom into a room-size rug and bind the edges. Then simply lay it on top of the floor as you would any carpet to give the appearance of a carpet without the potential for damage to your hardwood floor that exists with traditional wall-to-wall installation. You might even be able to find an inexpensive carpet remnant in a size that suits your needs and have it bound into a room-size rug. That will save you a lot of money and give you the appearance and soft surface of carpeting, but spare you the difficulties of removing it.

on your own

Install Carpet Tile

Another advancement in carpeting is carpet tile. They have come a long way from the depressing industrial-gray flat-weave squares found all too often in office cubicles. Carpet tiles are a great way to help transform a basement into a family or guest room or to quickly replace old carpeting with something hip and modern. And it's super-easy to do on your own.

Carpet tiles are easily installed and removed. If a square is damaged, you can simply pick it up and clean it or replace it with a new tile. The best part is that carpet tiles can be placed over wood, concrete, vinyl, or tile floors or plywood sub-floors without damaging them. One of the few materials you can't put them on top of is soft stuff like carpet padding and carpeting, unless you are using the squares to form an area rug.

How long will it take me? An average 8 × 10-foot room can be done in an afternoon! In less than 3 hours you can have a brand-new, cozy floor.

How much will it cost? Carpet tiles can run from $4 to $10 a square foot. You can cover an 8 × 10-foot room for less than $700.

What do I need? The carpet tiles, adhesive tabs supplied by the manufacturer, and just a few other items:

Tape measure

1 piece heavy cardboard cut to the size of the tile

24-inch carpenter's square or straightedge

Carpet knife with a sharp blade

How do I do it?

1. If you are installing the tiles over a plywood subfloor, make sure it is tight and flush. Use a level to check any area that looks uneven. Any irregularities greater than $\frac{1}{16}$ inch need to be leveled with a leveling compound, available at hardware stores. Follow the manufacturer's instructions.

If you are installing the tiles on a concrete floor, make sure it is dry and fully cured if recently poured. Under normal conditions it takes a floor about 90 days to cure. In existing slabs, cracks wider than $\frac{1}{16}$ inch should be patched and leveled with patching compound available at hardware stores. Follow the manufacturer's instructions—it's easy. If your floor is not sealed, seal it now with a nonsolvent-based concrete sealer, following the manufacturer's instructions. Failing to seal the floor can cause indoor air quality problems, so this is important, especially in basements.

2. Calculate the number of tiles you need. Manufacturers offer easy calculators that help determine how many squares you will need. But you must measure the floor area to be covered. Use a tape measure to find the size of the perimeter of the room. Always buy 10 percent more tiles than you think you'll need so you'll have replacement squares later on or in case you make cutting errors during installation.

3. Unpack and inspect the tiles. Let them acclimate to the room for 24 hours.

4. Find the center of the room and place your first tile. Typically only certain tiles need to be affixed, and those only with the adhesive tabs supplied by the manufacturer (don't use any adhesive other than that supplied or recommended by the manufacturer).

5. Work from the center outward by placing squares on each side of the first square. Keep working toward the perimeter of the room, butting the squares against each other. Use adhesive tabs to apply the first tile and every sixth or seventh tile after that, or follow the manufacturer's recommendations.

6. When you reach the perimeter, you may have to cut the tiles to fit. To mark the necessary cut, place the tile upside down and overlapping the adjoining tile so it fits against the wall. Mark the line where the tile meets the one already in place. Place the tile to be cut under a piece of heavy cardboard. Using a straightedge or carpenter's square as a guide to ensure that the line is straight, score the back of the carpet tile with the carpet knife. Make several gentle passes with the knife along the score line until you cut all the way through. Butt the cut edge of the tile against the wall. Use the adhesive tabs to secure the perimeter pieces.

barbara's best bet

EXCELSIOR! (EVER UPWARD!)

Don't forget the ceiling. Bumpy "popcorn" acoustic ceilings are outdated and unattractive. I have two friends who walked away from two great houses because they were so turned off by the popcorn ceilings.

That's too bad because they are easily removed with a scraper attached to a long pole (be sure to empty the room of furniture and cover the floor with a canvas drop cloth before you begin, and wear safety glasses). Yes, it's labor intensive and messy, but it's worth it.

ALL FOUR WALLS

I always say that if you understand the way a wall is built, you understand a lot about life. A wall doesn't stay up by itself—it needs a support system of studs and tracks for stability and permanence. Plus, you can do so many things with the walls around you, especially if they are made from drywall, which is smooth and easy to repair. You can even cover up damaged drywall by fastening an entirely new layer over it. Cover kitchen and bathroom walls with water-resistant high-gloss paint, glazed ceramic tile, or stone. Apply scrubbable paints to the walls in children's rooms. Apply a faux finish to the wall above your fireplace! Paint it, tile it, add molding—the list of possibilities is endless. Don't pass up the chance to put your personal decorating stamp on your walls to give your home life and personality.

MOLDINGS

Moldings in particular add so much architectural detail and presence to a room. Whenever I buy a house that has flat, narrow, "clamshell"-style molding around the windows and doors and as the baseboards, the first thing I do is replace it with wider, more detailed molding. Most people seem to love crown molding. It's a classic sign of quality construction and elegant, traditional style. Personally, I am not a fan of crown molding—I think it's slightly old-fashioned when installed in modern settings. Wide, luxurious baseboards are another story. They rock! They add substance and richness to a room. And it's the kind of detail that people always notice. I immediately replace conventional 2- or 3-inch baseboards with superwide 5- or 6-inch styles. Any way you look at it, adding simple, decorative molding to a plain room is a good aesthetic and financial investment.

go to the pros

ADD WIDE BASEBOARDS AND CROWN MOLDING

A wide baseboard grounds a room and adds architectural detail. Great moldings make a house seem more expensive and customized.

Who does it?

A carpenter. You can do it yourself, but wood moldings are expensive and unless you are comfortable making the sometimes intricate corner cuts or don't mind sacrificing some of the material you buy to errors, I would go with professional installation.

How long does it take?

In addition to the 48 hours the wood should sit in the room to acclimate to the environment, count on about 2 days to remove old molding and install new baseboards and crown molding in one large 16 x 20-foot room or two smaller (8 x 10) rooms.

How much will it cost?

Paintable pine or stainable oak baseboards can run from $5 to $10 a linear foot. Labor varies depending on region, but expect to pay about $2 per linear foot for installation. That means you can install molding in a large room for around $1,000. Ask for at least three bids—one that includes preparation (painting or staining) of the new moldings and baseboards and removal of the old materials and one for installation only. If you want to save some money, prepare the new moldings and remove the old ones yourself. It's easy to paint or stain molding before it's installed and to pry off old molding with the claw end of a hammer. Make sure the estimate includes installation of shoe molding—a quarter-round strip of wood that protects the baseboard from dinging by chair legs and shoes and provides a clean, finished appearance.

What happens?

The old baseboards and crown molding are removed. Then the installer cuts the new moldings to size and applies them with glue and finish nails. Make sure he or she taps the nails in with a nail set (so the wood does not get dented by the hammer); fills holes, corners, and seams with wood putty; and touches up marks with paint or stain. Also make sure shoe molding is installed.

—— on your own ——

Extend Existing Molding

If your house lacks substantial moldings and you can't or don't want to go to the expense of removing and replacing what's there, there's a simple and inexpensive trick you can use to make it appear as if your molding is wider than it really is. In fact, this deception is so sublimely realistic it should be illegal! You can beef up the size of window moldings and baseboards by placing strips of 1-inch half-round or picture frame molding 2 to 4 inches above baseboards, under crown molding, and all around existing window trim and then painting it, the original trim, and the space between the two the same color to create the illusion of wide trim. Half-round molding is not as expensive as real molding, and it's easier to cut, too.

How long will it take me? About 90 minutes to complete a window, including painting, and about half a day to add and paint baseboard or crown moldings in an 18 × 20-foot room.

How much will it cost? Picture frame molding or 1-inch flat trim costs less than $1 per linear foot.

What do I need? In addition to the molding, which you can have the local lumberyard or home improvement center cut to your specifications, you need the following:

Straightedge ruler

Pencil

Miter box and saw

Wood glue

1 box of 4D 1½-inch finish nails

Hammer

Wood putty (make sure it is paintable, if you are painting the molding instead of staining it)

Fine-grit sandpaper

Gloss paint

How do I do it?

1. Using a straightedge ruler and pencil, measure 2 inches out from the existing window trim, 3 or 4 inches above the baseboards, or 3 or 4 inches below the crown molding. Then measure the distance around the room and around the windows where you marked. Use the measurements to buy your molding; always get 10 percent more than you need to allow for possible cutting errors.

2. To extend window trim molding: Make 45-degree miter cuts in the molding to create a picture frame around each window you marked earlier. Attach the molding with wood glue and finish nails (one nail every 6 inches). Fill in any nail holes with wood putty. Sand lightly and paint the old trim, wall, and new trim to achieve the appearance of wide molding.

3. To extend baseboards or crown molding: Tack and glue the half-round strip where you marked above the baseboard all the way around the room. Butt strips together tightly to make the seams as unnoticeable as you can. Cut at a 45-degree angle and butt the ends together to meet at the corners. Fill in nail holes, seams, and corners with wood putty, sand lightly, and paint both old and new trim and the wall space between them for a unified look.

Tip: Try adding a narrow molding strip right next to the existing molding, using the directions above, for more dimension.

WINDOWS ON THE WORLD

A house would be pretty dismal without windows. They let in light and air and provide a view of the great outdoors (even if it's a city skyline). Windows also play a part in the integrity of the design and architecture of a house. The right windows, especially if they are part of a specific style of architecture, are worth saving. Plus, restoring windows is more cost-effective than replacing them. Older windows may have a lesser insulating effect (reported as an "R-value") than new windows, but the difference isn't that significant. For example, an older single-paned window has an R-value of 1, while most new double-glazed windows have an R-value of 3. That slight difference might not be worth the expense or damage to the architectural integrity of an older home. You can also seal gaps, replace weather stripping, install storm windows, and apply a good-quality low-e film to existing glass to make old windows function just as efficiently as new models. In short, quality windows add value to a home—at least 85 percent of the cost of replacement windows can be recouped through a higher resale price for your home. In some desirable housing markets, that percentage can exceed 100 percent.

go to the pros

RESTORE WINDOWS

If you live in an older home or apartment with unique windows, it's worth it to repair them. Old glass has a magical quality that is hard to replicate, and the style of older windows gives your home a custom look from inside and out. Since window sizes and styles have only been standardized in the last 50 years, old windows are unique! However, many development and tract houses built in the last 30 years don't include architecturally significant windows, so trying to save something that wasn't that good to begin with is a waste of money—you're probably better off replacing these windows (see page 81).

Who does it?

A window and sash restoration service. These professionals have carpentry skills and specialized knowledge about window glazing and glass cutting. An experienced handyperson or carpenter can also do the job—but make sure he or she has a lot of experience in working with windows. Either way, ask for references and view previous work.

How long does it take?

It can take several days or months to restore all the windows in your house. But count on 2 to 3 hours per window.

How much will it cost?

A window restoration expert can charge between $45 and $60 per hour.

What happens?

The restoration expert will evaluate the condition of your windows and then make recommendations. A price estimate follows. Once the restoration begins, expect total disassembly of the windows. Elements of a quality job include planing and sanding of the frames, which may help with operational difficulties caused by numerous coats of old paint; replacement of rope and chain sash mechanisms; and re-weighting. Sashes should not fall down or float up; they should be suspended in space. The restoration expert will also reinforce loose joints in the sashes. Caulking might be necessary to keep the joints from deteriorating any further. Epoxy restoration may be needed for badly rotted joints. You should expect installation of weather stripping for increased energy efficiency, lubrication of channels and pulleys to eliminate squeaks and sticking, and realignment of locks and stops. Stops are vertical strips of wood that control the bottom sash and are often held together by screws. Finally, the restorer will replace loose putty or caulk, replace any broken panes, and reglaze the glass.

$ barbara's best bet

WINDOW FILM

In summer, bright sun streaming through uncovered windows makes air conditioners work two to three times harder. You could draw the shades, but who likes spending time in a dark room on a gorgeous, sunny day? Instead, you can install a reflective window film over clear glass. It reduces cooling costs by 5 to 15 percent. Look for high-tech, spectrally selective film that permits daylight to enter your rooms while blocking solar heat. Most window film manufacturers offer warranties only with professional installation, but you can apply the film yourself. Professionally installed window films range from $1 to $5 per square foot.

on your own

Wash Your Windows

I am always astonished at how much more light comes in through clean windows as opposed to dingy ones. If you live in a city, you know how much grime and soot can impair your view. Even in the country, dirt and dust have a way of accumulating fast. Some newer double-hung windows pivot inward so you can wash the outside from indoors. If your windows don't do this or you have stationary or casement windows, you must wash the glass from the outside. Wash the exterior of windows at least twice a year, preferably on dry, sunny days in early fall and spring.

How long will it take me? Less than 3 hours

How much will it cost? Less than $10 in materials

What do I need? Not much:

Ladder

Garden hose with sprayer and 1-gallon liquid-distribution attachment

1 gallon white vinegar

Water

Large bucket

Old, clean T-shirts or lint-free sackcloth

Squeegee (optional)

Rubber gloves

Spray bottle filled with half vinegar and half water

How do I do it?

1. First, remove exterior screens or storm windows and use the hose and sprayer to wash them. Set them aside to dry.

2. Fill the liquid-distribution container with vinegar and attach it to the garden hose according to the manufacturer's instructions. It should allow you to reach the highest floors of your house. You can buy window cleaner in a bottle specifically designed to attach to a hose if you have a hard time finding a plain container designed for that application. Follow the manufacturer's instructions in this case.

3. Start spraying the upper-floor windows, replenishing the vinegar as needed. It will mix with the water as you spray.

4. When you are done, combine one part vinegar and one part water in a large bucket. Using a clean, old T-shirt or lint-free sackcloth, apply the solution to the outside of the windows on the lower floors in a circular motion. Use a squeegee to remove excess water.

5. When the exterior glass has been washed, rinse all the windows using the garden hose and sprayer.

6. Reinstall the dry screens.

7. Clean the interior side of the windows with a solution of half vinegar and half water in a spray bottle, again using a clean, old T-shirt or a piece of lint-free sackcloth in a circular motion.

$ barbara's best bet

SPREAD THE LIGHT AROUND

Once your windows are sparkling clean, consider painting your ceiling a bright white. It will reflect natural light better than off-white or a dark color, making the room seem brighter. If you have sliding glass doors or tall, narrow floor-to-ceiling windows (many Victorian houses have these kinds of windows), you can place freestanding or built-in bookshelves on either side of them. If the sides of the shelves are painted a bright, reflective color such as white or cream, light reflects off the sides and bounces into the room. Semigloss paint intensifies the reflective quality. Add a shelf above the doors or windows to tie the shelves together and reflect and diffuse even more light.

go to the pros

REPLACE AND ADD NEW WINDOWS

Most of us love light, so replacing small windows with larger ones or with sliding glass doors is a huge asset. Installing windows where there are none is also a great way to brighten a dark space, including hallways and bathrooms. In very large spaces, where the perimeter walls may be far from the actual living spaces, the center of a great room can seem dim indeed. In older homes, small rooms feel claustrophobic without adequate light from outside. New windows and skylights bring in more natural light, which can cut back on electricity consumption during daylight hours.

Who does it?

The window supplier will send trained installers who have the specific carpentry skills needed to mount your new windows.

How long does it take?

It takes about an hour for an experienced pro to put in a window.

How much will it cost?

Prices vary depending on the size of the window—large custom picture windows can cost upwards of $1,000 apiece with installation. Small skylights or standard-size double-hung windows can cost $250 to $500 installed.

What happens?

The supplier will visit your house and discuss options with you. Once you've decided what you want, he or she will supply you with an estimate that should include the window itself, cutting an opening or removing the old window and enlarging the opening, and installing and trimming out the new window. A good installer will also replace any window hardware, such as blinds, when he or she is done.

WINDOW STYLES

Whatever style of home you have, you can find a window for it. Manufacturers make standard sizes, but in a huge variety of shapes (round, rectangular, square, and octagonal, to name a few) and styles (traditional, modern). Custom windows further widen the choice—you can design your own for a truly unique style statement. Always consider the style of your home and how the windows will look from the outside when you make your choice. Here are some options and their uses.

Skylights

Skylights are so popular that I am going to spend a little more time discussing them. A skylight is the best choice for increasing natural light in areas such as bedrooms where the ceiling is steeply sloped, as in a Cape Cod–style house. Adding a skylight is less expensive than having a dormer window built. Rooms that offer no interesting views or where privacy would be an issue if you were to put in a standard window are good candidates for a skylight. Rooms in which storage is a real priority may also benefit from a skylight since it will not require you to sacrifice wall space. A skylight can bring more sunlight into a dark, north-facing room.

In rooms with a sloped ceiling, place skylights close to the walls for the same reason you would place a window near a side wall: to bounce light around the room. When placing skylights in the middle of a ceiling, consider installing two skylights parallel to each other instead of one large skylight. That will introduce and diffuse sunlight better. Remember, too, that it is hard to control the light that comes through skylights. A skylight I put in the middle of the ceiling in one of my guest rooms made it difficult for guests to sleep in late. The solution: a manual or remotely controlled powered retractable blind.

As with standard windows, buy the very best skylight you can afford and have it installed by a professional. It is imperative that skylights be tightly sealed to guard against weather leaks. A roof insulates a house and a skylight puts a hole in that insulation, so the glass should be triple-glazed, if possible.

An alternative to a skylight is a solar tube or tubular skylight. These reflective tunnels run from the roof surface into any given space. They are perfect for bringing the sunshine into a walk-in closet, bathroom, second- or third-floor hallway or stairwell, or utility room. A diffuser on the ceiling end helps to bounce the light around the space, so you don't have a narrow circle of light beamed into the room. Several brands are available, most of which are inexpensive and certainly less costly than a standard skylight.

Double-Hung

This is the most traditional, common window style. The top and bottom sashes of the window slide up and down to close and open. Modern windows pivot in for easy cleaning of the outside. You can order this style with each sash having a single or multiple sections of glass, called *lights*. Multiple-light windows are more traditional.

Casement

Casement windows are a good choice for modern homes. They crank open to the side and when closed leak less air than traditional double-hung windows because the casement sash compresses against the frame.

Sliding Windows and Sliding Glass Doors

Sliding windows and doors offer an expansive view. Sliding windows and doors have a contemporary flavor when they are made with large pieces of glass and a more traditional look if they have multiple lights (some sliders have molding applied to the surface of the glass to give the appearance of individual panes of glass).

comfort zone

A PLACE FOR EVERY WINDOW

Placement is important—a new window must be situated so that it brings in good light and a pleasing view and blends well with adjacent windows from the inside and the outside of the house. I think it is better to place a window near an adjacent wall so that the wall can act as a reflector, spreading the light farther. Windows that must be centrally located should be tall so that the ceiling can act as a reflecting surface to increase the penetration of daylight into the space. If you are placing the window on the south side of your house, consider putting an awning over it or protecting it with trees or shrubs. Otherwise, you may have harsh light streaming in that will heat up the room during the summer.

Greenhouse

Windows can take the shape of a greenhouse box built into your wall. They jut out to let your plants enjoy the sunshine while you enjoy a lush, green view.

Block

Glass or acrylic block windows let in light where privacy is an issue, such as a bathroom or a wall in very close proximity to a neighbor's house. In addition, glass or acrylic blocks can be used for walls, partitions, and window or door sidelights in large rooms to delineate space while still letting light through.

Picture

A bay or picture window lets you enjoy a great view through an expanse of glass. You need to make sure you have enough space on the exterior of your house before you have one installed because a bay window projects out at a 30-, 45-, or 90-degree angle. A bay window design can also include sections that open, allowing for many ventilation options.

Bow windows are similar to bay windows, but they form a smooth outward curve. They're often made up of a series of other window styles, such as fixed, casement, or double-hung. In the sill area, you can put a window seat or a large shelf for displaying plants.

Traditional picture windows are generally large rectangular windows, often stationary, that can frame beautiful views. Tempered glass panels can also be used to create dramatic all-glass corners, which is a wonderful way to frame particularly special views. In other words, the two flat panels of glass actually become the walls. It's a very modern look that is not appropriate for all house styles.

Transom

Transom windows can be added to existing or combined with new standard windows for increased ventilation. A transom window placed above or below a picture window, for instance, will expand the view and increase the flow of fresh air. Transom windows are also a great accent over doors.

DOOR STORY

Have you ever really looked at the doors in your house or condo? What are they made of? What do the doorknobs look like? Are the hinges attractive and functional? Do the doors operate smoothly and close tightly or do they stick or even refuse to fit into the doorjamb? Doors can be overlooked in a home, yet they are so essential for establishing privacy and controlling sound.

Hollow-core doors are the least expensive type of door; therefore, many builders use them in tract and development homes. After I replaced the clamshell molding in my first house, I replaced the hollow-core doors with solid paneled doors. Hollow-core doors do not control noise and have a tendency to expand and contract. They can also be unattractive. Can you tell I don't like them?

Solid wood or solid-core interior doors add value to a home because they are an appearance upgrade—they add architecture and custom style. They also provide good soundproofing and are sturdy in the face of wear and tear.

——— on your own ———

Replace a Door

If your house has unattractive or just plain boring interior doors, it's not that difficult to change them yourself if they are of a standard size and the doorjambs are in good shape. If doorjambs need to be replaced, call in a carpenter unless you are a very experienced handywoman (or handyman!) or are willing to give a difficult project a try. You can find information about replacing doorjambs at home improvement stores, which often offer free lessons and clinics.

How long will it take me? Less than 2 hours

How much will it cost? A standard solid wood interior paneled door with pre-drilled holes costs between $50 and $75 at a home improvement center. Special woods or unique styles could cost more.

What do I need? Doors come either blank or predrilled. A blank door means you have to drill your own holes for the doorknob and lock. Predrilled doors already have the doorknob and lock holes drilled. If you are just replacing the door itself, measure the existing door and purchase a predrilled door that will fit into the existing doorjamb. The door frame (the structure that supports the door), the door-jamb (the vertical sides of the frame), and the existing trim remain intact. In addition to the new door, you will also need:

Screwdriver

Hammer

Wood plane (may not be necessary,
but have one on hand just in case)

Utility knife

Pencil

Sandpaper block

Hinges

Beautiful new doorknobs—
here's your chance to really dress things up!

How do I do it?

1. Remove the old door by pulling or gently tapping out the hinge pins with a hammer and separating them. Remove the hinges and door-knobs from the door.

2. Use the old door as a pattern by laying it on top of the new door. Use the hinge edge of the old door to line up the doors. This will let you know if the top, bottom, or doorknob edge of the new door needs to be trimmed to fit the door frame. Make a note of how long the original door is. It may have been trimmed at some point. If there was a large gap at the bottom of the old door, you may not have to trim the new door as much for it to fit. If the new door needs to be trimmed slightly, do this with a wood plane.

3. Mark any edges that do not match the outline of the old door with a utility knife or pencil. Remove the excess material with a sandpaper block or a wood plane if the amount is small. Trimming should be minor if the new door is of the same standard size as the old one. Go slowly and be conservative, checking the size again after every pass.

4. Add hinges to the new door, using the old door as a pattern for their placement.

5. Attach the new doorknobs by following the manufacturer's instructions.

6. Rehang the door. If the door sticks, mark the sticky spot, pull the pins from the hinges, remove the door, and sand or plane the spot until the door swings freely when rehung.

Now that you're done sprucing up the finishes
all around your house, I bet you're thinking you could use
a little more space. Who doesn't want a little more room
to move around in? In the next chapter I tell you
how to plan and prepare for an addition. Read on.

!

CHAPTER 5

Adding On

Doesn't everyone want more space at home, whether it's for relaxing, entertaining, working, or just storing extra gear? Expanding the size of your home also happens to be one of the best ways to increase its value. Space sells! More of it increases the value of your house by 50 to 100 percent *over* what you paid to have the work done. When I bought my first house, it seemed like a natural extension (literally) to add three bedrooms and two bathrooms, create a more lucrative income-producing property, and eventually be able to sell a six-bedroom, four-bathroom home instead of the three-bedroom, two-bathroom home that I originally purchased.

Transforming unfinished space into a usable, comfortable room is a good place to start. Adding on a brand-new wing or extension is even better. What do you need— room for an office so you can work from home? Space for a children's playroom? Do you dream of having an at-home spa? Adding space to an existing home is one way of making your dreams come true! There's nothing more fun or rewarding than planning to add on to your already beautiful home. When I was a kid, I used to toy with the idea of creating different shapes and sizes of houses and rooms using building blocks.

Today, when I actually add on to a blueprint of the existing floor plan and then watch the drawing come to life, it is always a fulfilling and exciting experience. Getting a good architect is imperative to setting your sights on a bigger space. Designs can be altered on paper in many different ways, and an architect will help you refine that vision for maximum function and style before any ground is broken.

If you live in a condo and think this chapter isn't for you, think again. You can buy the apartment next to yours, break through the separating wall, and turn a studio into a one-bedroom pad. Or you can buy the unit above yours, break through the ceiling, build a staircase, and turn an apartment into a swanky duplex with a master suite. It's the same process as adding a room to a freestanding house. Why not dream big? If I can do it, so can you!

GROW THE SPACE YOU HAVE

Transforming existing raw space into an extra bedroom, a playroom, or a guest or master suite is an affordable way to make your house bigger. You can also winterize an unheated sunroom or porch to transform a two- or three-season room into a year-round retreat. You can transform a two-bedroom, two-bath house into a "new" three-bedroom, three-bathroom house just by making your unused space livable!

BE YOUR OWN PROJECT MANAGER

Finishing the existing raw space in your home for livability requires the help of specialists in several trades: plumbing, carpentry, electrical, and others, including flooring and possibly stoneworking for tile work. So while it's not a do-it-yourself job, you can manage the project yourself and become your own general contractor. That way, you'll save money and choose and work with the tradespeople whom you really like. Managing the project gives you tremendous control over personnel, quality control, and finishes. You're the boss! Here are the basic steps you'll want to follow:

Set aside some time

Expect to spend from 1 to several hours a day for several months dealing with some aspect of the renovation. Managing the transformation of any space in your home does not require you to be on-site every minute, but you do have to check in often, inspect the work as it progresses, pay bills, consult with the tradespeople who are on the site, coordinate with and schedule the tradespeople who need to come in, make sure the site is organized safely and in a way that protects workers (and therefore your liability), monitor rubbish removal, and troubleshoot.

Determine your budget

Every decision you make flows from your budget, from how much to spend on flooring to how fancy you want your bathroom fixtures to be.

Decide how you want to use the space

Will it be an extra bedroom and bath, a family room, or a children's playroom? The function will help inform many of the finishes you choose. For example, a children's playroom may benefit from a hardwood floor partially covered by a large rug. How elaborate do you want the bathroom to be? If you are transforming a space into a master suite, the bathroom should have double vanities and a glass enclosure for the shower, which should have extra wall and overhead showerheads.

Gather the right professionals

Several professionals are involved in an addition project. They include:

Architect

Carpenter and/or drywall contractor

Flooring contractor

Licensed electrician

HVAC specialist

Licensed plumber

Window supplier/installer

As project manager, you coordinate the work, schedule, and budget. Jobs need to be completed in a particular order. Follow this general timeline:

Prepare the floor

Check the condition of the existing subfloor and floor joists. If you are finishing a basement, you must inspect the condition of its floor. Most basements have poured concrete floors, and sometimes they slope steeply for drainage purposes. If that's the case, the floor must be leveled before proceeding with the work. A handyperson or contractor should pour a thin concrete overlay to level it. Be sure that access to any existing floor drains is maintained! Drains need to stay functional in case of basement flooding. Check with a plumber to find out if you will be required to periodically pour water in them to prevent sewer gas from building up.

Install any necessary HVAC systems

Ductwork is cumbersome. In basements, where ceiling height is always a consideration, soffits may be required to cover up any vents running overhead, which can lower the ceiling. Basements are usually cool and may not require air-conditioning systems. They do require heating, however. Be sure the HVAC specialist locates supply ducts near outside walls. Install return air ducts on interior walls or ceilings away from the supply ducts. The idea is to "draw" air across the room. Particular attention must be paid to ventilating, heating, and cooling attic rooms.

Install plumbing

You can solve plumbing issues in other parts of your house at this time, too, if necessary. If the existing drain stacks in the house are made from PVC, they need to be wrapped with insulation to minimize sound transmission. Cold-water lines may need to be insulated if you have had problems in the past with condensation, because it may drip onto your new ceiling. Have the plumber *rough in* bathroom plumbing so he or she can come back later to install the fixtures. *Rough* plumbing is all the plumbing components that need to be installed before the finish tradespeople (drywall contractor, painter, and so on) come in to do their jobs, including the waste and supply water lines that are in the walls or framing of the building. Ask the plumber to use $1/2$-inch or 1-inch lines instead of the more common $1/4$-inch lines in the bathroom for extra water pressure.

Have necessary electrical work done

All electrical work must be done in compliance with the National Electrical Code or the code adopted by your community. Don't skimp on the electrical system. Make a list of everything you intend to use in the room (appliances, light fixtures, electronic equipment, and so on) so the electrician can calculate the required load and make sure you have enough circuits. He or she can rough in wiring for ceiling fixtures at this time and come back to install the fixtures when the drywall or drop ceiling has been installed. Think ahead. Make sure you can access the main electrical service panel and telephone and cable TV termination points. Ask the electrician to install conduits through which additional wires can be run at a later date. Don't forget about wiring the space for surround sound.

Install cable and phone lines

Call your service companies and schedule a time for them to add new telephone, data, and cable wiring. Be sure to have them add extra phone and data lines now, even if you don't plan on using them all right away. Adding them later on is more expensive.

Build and insulate the walls

A carpenter can install 2 × 4-inch studs if they aren't already there, as well as a variety of thermal insulation materials, from traditional soft batting to rigid foil-faced sheets to blown-in insulation. He or she should be able to advise you on what is recommended for your geographic region and application.

Install walls

You can choose one of several types of wallboard or paneling. I prefer drywall because it gives you the most flexibility and doesn't scream "finished basement" the way paneling does. Plus, you can always apply bead-board wainscoting, faux finishes, wallpaper, or other treatments over drywall at a later date.

Install new or additional windows and doors

See pages 81 and 85 for ideas.

Install the ceiling

I prefer drywall ceilings, but I admit that the ubiquitous and industrial-looking acoustical tile or drop ceiling has come a long way. It now comes in a variety of styles, from bead board to decorative embossed styles that look like old-fashioned tin ceilings. The advantages of installing a drop ceiling are that it creates an accessible tray for ductwork and wiring and if one tile gets damaged, it's easy to replace (buy 10 percent more than you need for coverage). The disadvantages are that it lowers the ceiling height, which might be at a premium in your attic or basement. For a drywall ceiling, the drywall contractor or carpenter builds soffits around any ductwork. That means that making a drywall ceiling takes extra work and is therefore somewhat more expensive than a drop ceiling, but the ceiling will be lower only in the areas where ductwork exists and headroom is maximized everywhere else.

Install the floor

I love hardwood, as you know. If you happen to be finishing a basement-level room, however, think twice before choosing hardwood flooring. Hardwood flooring trade associations and manufacturers caution against using traditional hardwood below ground level, even in very dry basements. Instead, consider engineered hardwood click flooring, laminates, tile, or carpeting. If you are worried about wet floors or insect infestation, install treated or marine plywood as a subfloor before proceeding with the final finish.

Install final fixtures

Have the plumber and electrician return to install the permanent bathroom and electrical fixtures.

Paint trim and walls

Furnish your new rooms and enjoy them!

CREATE A NEW SPACE

Adding a room or an entire wing of a house means major construction, and that's not something I can take care of with my own two hands. A team of professionals and skilled tradesmen and tradeswomen is necessary to make a job like that a success. I have always acted as general contractor on building projects, hiring and supervising all the people who work on the job. Remember, as the home owner, you're the top dog even if you do hire a general contractor to manage a project. Everyone ultimately answers to you!

When I added new bedrooms and bathrooms to my first house, it was a big project, but I kept it simple. I did not add elaborate saunas or whirlpool tubs to the bathrooms or fancy finishes to the bedrooms. I just wanted great wood floors, basic but high-quality fixtures, high ceilings, lots of closets, and high-quality overall construction. Turning a standard three-bedroom house into a six-bedroom property was the right choice for the community, too. I could rent it out to summer people and eventually sell it as a viable rental property or large family home (and that's what I did just a few years later). Be mindful of your neighborhood. You don't want to overbuild, but you want to keep up with what your neighbors are doing. In general, bedrooms and bathrooms are always desirable add-ons, but adding on or extending family rooms and kitchens makes sense, too. Remember, high functionality equals high value. What new room or rooms would benefit you and your house the most?

KEEP TRACK

It is essential that you keep track of your expenses and stick as close as you can to your original budget. All receipts should be kept in a box to document expenditures. A written record will also help you keep track of every facet of your project, all in one easy place. Keep it on a clipboard in an obvious place so you never lose it. Using a brightly colored clipboard will help you distinguish it from the other items that are likely to pile up on desks and counters during any construction project.

IMPROVEMENTS AND ADDITIONS

DATE	DONE BY (NAME AND CONTACT INFO)
GRAND TOTAL:	

	DATE COMPLETED	ESTIMATED COST	ACTUAL COST

go to the pros

HIRE AN ARCHITECT

After a licensed surveyor confirms the boundaries of your property (you don't want to incur additional construction costs and possibly legal fees by accidentally building on your neighbor's property), the next person you need to hire when you're planning an addition is a registered architect. Everything flows from the plans he or she bases on your needs, desires, and budget. Every architect has a unique style—there are so many ways you can go. Postmodern, retro, traditional—the list goes on and on. In new builds, you can be as adventurous as your imagination and local building codes allow. With add-ons, you want to make sure the architect uses your ideas and proposed budget to come up with a plan that is in harmony with the existing house style.

Who are these people?

A registered architect is a person who plans, designs, and possibly oversees the construction of buildings and additions. They are different from designers, who are not regulated in the same way. Architects do not build houses, although they do sometimes own design-and-build companies. They supervise the construction to make sure their plans are being properly executed.

Where do I find them?

The best way to find an architect is through recommendations from friends or neighbors who have had work done that you like. Interview three architects, look at their past work, and then make a judgment based on that information. Better yet, drive around your town and look at the various projects that have been designed recently (and the materials that have been used in their construction). See anything you like? If so, stop and ask who designed the property. If you're unable to get any personal recommendations, check with the American Institute of Architects (AIA) for a list of registered architects in your area. If you are adding on to a historic home, check with your local historical society or historic zoning board for recommendations.

What kind of training and certification do they need?

Professional architects have completed extensive university coursework to earn a degree in architecture, design, and perhaps even engineering. They also have completed lengthy internships with an experienced architect or large architectural firm and passed a series of rigorous exams in order to be licensed. Look for the initials "RA" (Registered Architect) in conjunction with an architect's name. Verify the architect's licensing and other credentials by calling the AIA and the licensing board in your community (or in the community where the architect has an office).

How do I hire one?

Call at least three prospective registered architects and ask if they would be interested in working with you on a project. Give them some details on the scope of the project so they have an idea of the size. Always ask if they charge a fee for an initial interview; some architects do and some don't, but whether or not they charge is not an indication of their quality. When you meet with them, the first question you should ask each one is if he or she is the person who will actually work on your project. If not, ask to meet that person. If you are meeting with an architect at a large firm, be sure to ask if there will be more than one person assigned to your project and ask to meet the entire team. You will be spending a lot of time with your architect, so you should be sure you enjoy working with him or her. Trust your instincts—do you feel a connection? Does he or she understand and relate to what you envision for your home?

Next, determine what the architect's design philosophy and favorite styles are. Ask each one how long he or she thinks the project will take to complete and discuss fees and anticipated construction costs. An architect's fee can range from 10 to 15 percent of the total construction cost. They can also charge by the square footage of the design, or may just quote you a flat fee. I prefer being charged by the square foot or paying a flat fee. Ask for references from past clients and call them! Visit at least one project by your prospective architect.

Ask for a bid and make sure it includes a schedule of finishes. Sometimes the registered architect does the design but does not specify finishes or "call out" the style numbers and manufacturer's names of the different plumbing and lighting fixtures, and the latter is considered extra work. It's something you can do yourself, but it is very time-consuming.

I have accepted a bid—now what?

The design process starts. The architect you choose will come up with a set of floor plans and architectural drawings, and sometimes even engineered drawings depending on your local building codes and requirements, to secure work permits. He or she will also put an RA stamp on the final drawings to indicate that he or she is registered or licensed to practice. That's important for when you and the architect apply for building permits. The community office that issues permits wants to see that the drawings were done by an RA. If you are expanding an apartment building, you will also need a set of stamped plans to get approval from the condo or co-op board.

What's in the contract?

The contract your architect draws up should include the following items:

☐ The title and address of the project

☐ A description of services to be provided by the architect

☐ A description of the method of payment agreed upon by both parties

☐ The name, address, and license number of the architect and the name and address of the client

☐ A description of how additional services or changes to the plan will be handled by the architect and the client

☐ A description of how either party can terminate the contract, including how the final payment will be calculated in the event of termination

☐ A project schedule

☐ An estimated construction budget and a description of what it includes, along with contingencies for delays and changes

☐ A description of how the client will approve work so that the architect can proceed to the next phase

☐ A list of reimbursable expenses and descriptions of the procedures for authorization and compensation

☐ A schedule of when fee payments are due and in what amounts

☐ The amount of any required retainer fee and a description of how, when, and where it will be applied to the total fee for services

☐ A clarification of who is responsible for keeping project account records and when they may be reviewed

☐ A description of the procedure for handling disputes that may arise between the parties

Once the architect completes an acceptable plan, what happens?

If you hired the architect to design an addition and draw up a set of plans to be executed by a builder, his or her job is done unless there are problems with the plan discovered only after construction has begun and it needs to be revised. The architect should make the necessary adjustment as part of your agreement. However, if you make changes based on changing needs and desires, expect to pay your architect an extra fee. If it is convenient, many architects will visit the site to see how the project is progressing. If the property is far from their office, expect to pay their expenses for visits to the site. If you have hired an architect to manage the project, including hiring the builder (which I do not recommend; it is better to keep the architect and builder separate and have them report to you), he or she will visit the project and work with the builder until the job is done to your satisfaction. Architects can also troubleshoot with the builder on the design, no matter who hired the builder.

What should be on the architect's plan?

The blueprint for your home or addition should include layouts for floor plans, exterior and interior elevations, details, cross-section diagrams, and general notes explaining how your home or addition will be constructed. The blueprint package that architects supply usually contains six sheets. If you are adding a single room, some of these items may not be included:

1. Cover sheet. Shows a sketch or drawing of your finished home

2. Exterior elevation. Shows the front, rear, and sides of your house drawn in $\frac{1}{4}$-inch or $\frac{1}{8}$-inch scale

3. Foundation plans. Shows the complete foundation layout, including support walls, excavated and unexcavated areas, and foundation details

4. Detailed floor plans. Shows the layout of individual floors of your home in $\frac{1}{4}$-inch scale. All room features, such as window and door locations, electrical outlets, and switch locations, are included. Many other symbols may also appear, the meanings of which are detailed under "How do I read a blueprint?," below.

5. House sections. Shows sections of the foundation, interior walls, exterior walls, floors, and roof in a large-scale cutaway view, normally scaled at $\frac{1}{4}$ inch equals 1 foot, but it can also be scaled at $\frac{3}{8}$ or $\frac{1}{2}$ inch equals 1 foot. Additional cross-sections show changes in floor, ceiling, or roof heights in the relationship of one level to another. These sections show how the parts, rooms, staircases, and hallways of the house fit together.

6. Interior elevation. Shows the design, details, and layout of kitchen and bathroom cabinets and appliances, laundry room and mudroom areas, fireplaces, built-in book-cases, and other features.

How do I read a blueprint?

Once you understand what the universal symbols mean, you will be able to read any blueprint, anytime, anywhere. The blueprint symbols shown here are the generally accepted universal shorthand of architects, builders, and contractors. Your architect may have some "symbol quirks" and use variations on what is shown here, so ask him or her about any mark you do not understand.

Also note that in kitchen plans, the direction that appliance doors and interior doors swing should be included on blueprints because they help you visualize the flow of the space and can flag a potentially tight squeeze or awkward design.

ARCHITECTURAL BLUEPRINT KEY

To give you an idea of how these symbols work on an actual blueprint, I've provided sample architectural drawings from my own home renovations. On the next few pages, you'll see floor plans and partial elevations. What you won't see here are the detailed plumbing and electrical plans, but I've still provided a key to some common symbols. Plumbing and electrical schematics are particularly complex, so your builder or architect should provide you with his or her own key. Also, let me remind you that there are variations and exceptions to the standard symbols. The key below will get you started, but it is by no means a complete resource. You can find additional interpretations of standard architectural symbols by conducting a simple online search.

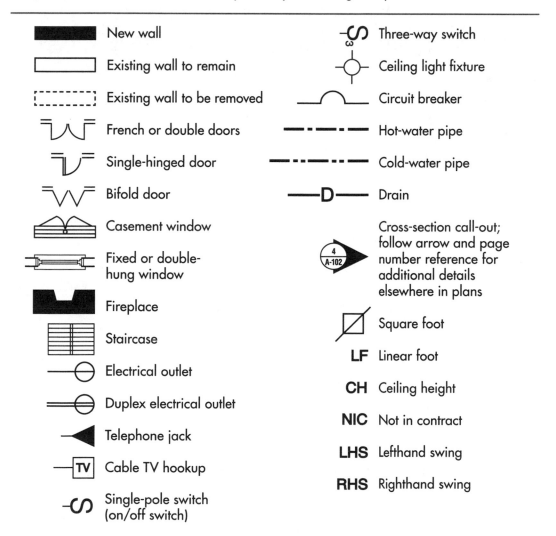

New wall	Three-way switch
Existing wall to remain	Ceiling light fixture
Existing wall to be removed	Circuit breaker
French or double doors	Hot-water pipe
Single-hinged door	Cold-water pipe
Bifold door	Drain
Casement window	Cross-section call-out; follow arrow and page number reference for additional details elsewhere in plans
Fixed or double-hung window	Square foot
Fireplace	LF Linear foot
Staircase	CH Ceiling height
Electrical outlet	NIC Not in contract
Duplex electrical outlet	LHS Lefthand swing
Telephone jack	RHS Righthand swing
Cable TV hookup	
Single-pole switch (on/off switch)	

FIRST FLOOR PLAN

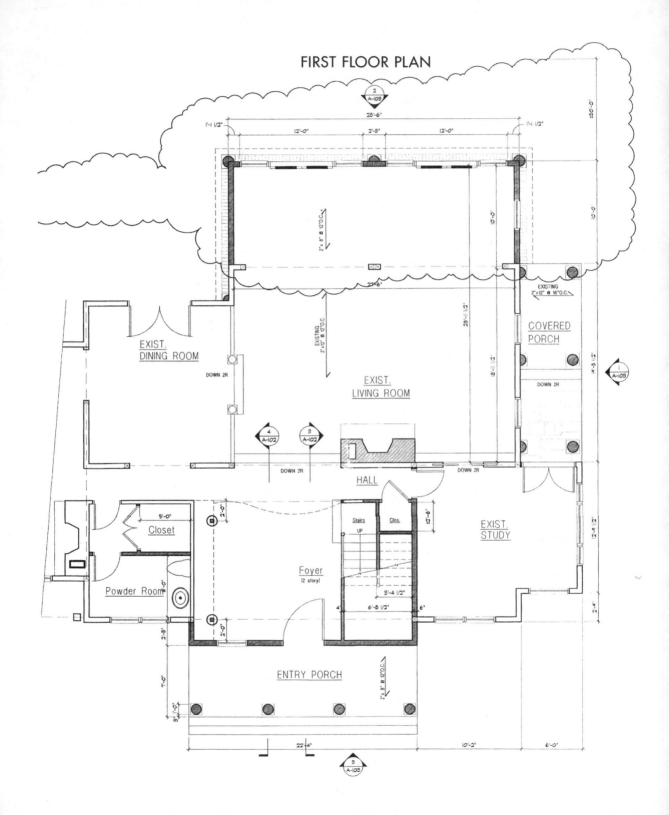

SECOND FLOOR PLAN

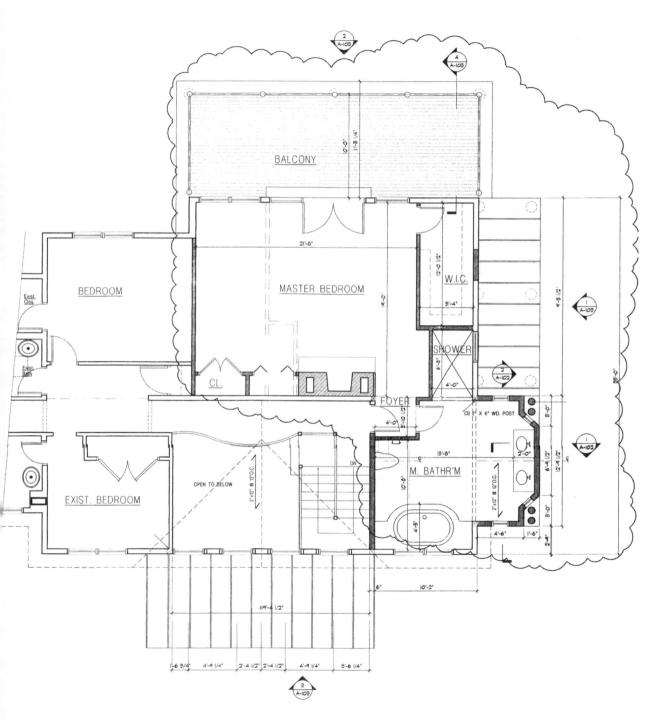

REAR ELEVATION WALL SECTION

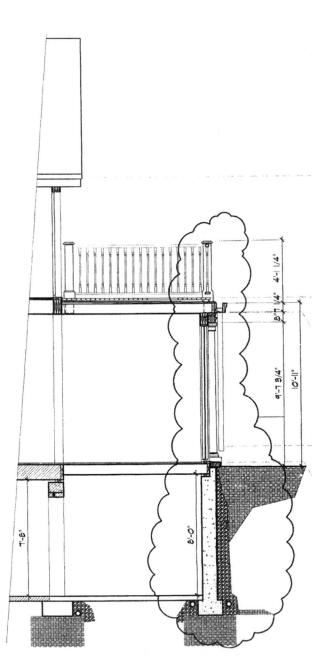

PARTIAL FRONT ELEVATION

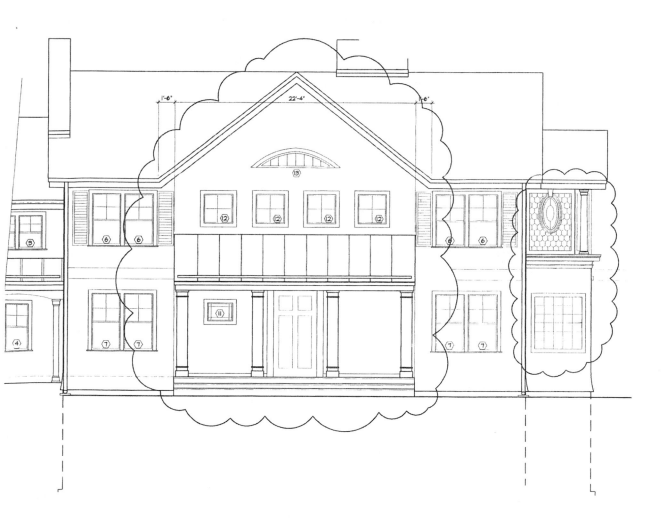

GETTING A VARIANCE

A variance is basically permission from local zoning authorities to build a structure or use a structure for something that is expressly prohibited by the current zoning laws. The best-laid architectural plans won't do you a bit of good if the town you live in won't let you execute them. Check with your municipality to find out what is required before you start on the job. They will tell you exactly what they need to see to issue permits and variances. In some towns, the process takes a few weeks, but it can take months to process a variance. Take that into consideration and apply early.

There are times when a community will not grant a variance. If you live in a designated historical district, there may be strict rules on everything from modification of buildings to what color you paint your house or mailbox. If you live in such an area, you will have to have a public hearing to determine if your plans fall within the historical guidelines set by the town, and then secure approval from a committee.

If a community requires owners to adhere to particular construction standards, like East Hampton, New York, does, it should supply them with documentation detailing those rules. A local architect should be familiar with these rules. Also make sure that you can add the number of square feet you want to; some towns limit the size of a house in relation to the lot's size. For example, you may not be able to put anything larger than a 3,000-square-foot house on a half-acre lot.

Another situation in which strict rules on modifying and building apply is when the site is on or near wetlands. For example, my friends Connie and Bill wanted to extend their small house, which was near a stream. They applied for a variance, but it was denied. They could not extend the house past its original footprint. They could only build upward, which they did get permission to do. Their project proceeded, but they needed to have new plans drawn up.

Clearing land could also be an issue. Some towns will not permit you to clear all trees or foliage from the property, only a certain percentage. Fines will be applied if you exceed the limit. You do not want to take the risk.

A variance may also be necessary if your property has some unique characteristic, such as a severe slope or an odd shape, that prevents you from enjoying the same kind of use of your property that your neighbors have. You can request variances for building height, fence heights, building locations, and setbacks.

To apply for a variance, you complete an application and submit it to your town's planning and building services department. Every municipality is different, of course, but as part of the application process, many require you to submit the appropriate number of copies of the following:

- [ ] Application forms and initial site and project description

- [ ] Architect's plans

- [ ] Survey or map of your property

- [ ] Architectural drawings, including elevations

- [ ] Filing fee

You will be notified by mail of the time and place that your application will be considered. Public notice of the hearing for your application will be published in a local newspaper, and the owners of adjoining properties will be notified of the application. Obviously you'll want to attend this hearing, and your architect should also attend.

If you are turned down, you can always make an appeal. Typically there is a predetermined period, usually 10 to 14 days after the decision has been made, to file your appeal. If your application is approved but you're unhappy with any conditions attached to the variance, you can appeal them. Appeals generally must be filed in writing, accompanied by yet another filing fee.

go to the pros

HIRE A BUILDER

You're well on your way to getting the home of your dreams. If you hired the architect to act as project manager, you do not need to hire a general contractor; however, you do need to hire a builder. You can find an architect/builder to take care of both planning and construction, but I think it is best to keep the two jobs separate. Experience has shown me that the process works best when there are different tiers of authority and delegation. The home owner is the top dog, the architect oversees the construction specifications, and the builder and his or her tradespeople do the actual hands-on construction.

Who are these people?

A builder is the person who follows the architect's plans for construction.

Where do I find them?

Your architect can recommend builders whom he has worked with successfully. Put them at the top of your list. You can also ask friends and neighbors for recommendations. Your neighborhood is a builder's showcase. If you are still having trouble finding the right person, you can contact your state's Home Builders Association for a list of pros in your area.

What kind of training and certification do they need?

You'll want to find a builder with a long-standing good reputation in your community. Look for someone who is either a Registered Builder or Registered Remodeler and belongs to a Home Builders Association. This indicates that the builder has met certain standards and educational requirements. A Registered Builder or Remodeler may or may not have had formal school training, but he or she will have apprenticed under a master builder for many years.

In addition, it is essential that the builder be insured. Ask for a copy of the policy and of his or her workers' compensation policies. Insist that your name be listed as an "additional insured" on the builder's policies. If someone gets hurt on the job, the builder's insurance company will pay the bills. If the builder balks at this, hire someone else. It is necessary and expected. Make sure you have copies of each contractor's workers' compensation policies in your hand before work begins. Ensure that the policies are authentic by calling the policy provider and verifying that the policy is valid. I hate to say this, but some people falsify such forms.

What else do I need to do?

Ask for references and call them. Visit homes and additions the builder has worked on and talk to the owners. Were the builder and his or her crew neat and respectful? Did they do high-quality work? Were problems addressed soon after they happened? Make sure there are no bad reports from consumer affairs groups. Finally, make sure all the tradespeople you want to hire have home improvement licenses. Some municipalities require this.

The paperwork is in order—what comes next?

Get three or more detailed, written estimates. Request that all tasks be included in the bids, including demolition, trash removal, and finishing work. When you get all three bids, compare them. Are they similar? If the bids are within 10 to 15 percent of each other, the estimates are most likely a fair reflection of the going rate for work in your area. Base your hiring decision on your instinct about the people. Who had the best references? Which one showed up on time and got back to you promptly with a bid?

If one of the bids is much lower than the other two (30 percent or more), it's probably too good to be true. If one bid is much higher than the others, it might be a sign that the builder is having money problems or is trying to take advantage of you.

I have accepted a bid—what should I do now?

Draw up a contract specifying:

Work to be done

Cost estimate

Payment schedule. Limit deposits or up-front payments to material costs only. Ask for receipts before paying for additional materials.

Materials to be used for the project. This should include the brand name and model number of specific fixtures and installed equipment (you don't want to pay for one kind of window and end up with another!) and even paint colors.

Start and estimated completion dates

What's the building process, in general?

Before building begins, you have to file the approved set of architectural documents with the local building department and apply for a permit to build. Once the permit is approved, you must post the permit where people can clearly see it on the property and then you can start to build. Don't even think about adding an addition illegally; you will be fined by the town. Moreover, selling a house with an illegal addition can be difficult and, at the very least, can jeopardize the value of your property.

$ barbara's best bet

LOVE THY NEIGHBOR (SO THY NEIGHBOR LOVES YOU BACK)

Once you have permission to build, I recommend very strongly that you tell your neighbors about the work before it begins. Assure them that you have all the necessary permits and permissions in order and that work will only occur during permitted times (for example, most towns do not allow work to be done during certain times of day or on Sundays). Show them you care about their privacy and well-being. When the work is done, throw a party and invite them. Thank them for being so patient. If there are problems with the neighbors, try to resolve them as quickly as possible. Remember, property-line disputes can be avoided completely by using an accurate survey.

Sometime after construction begins, a building inspector will show up a total of three times, once for an electrical inspection, once again for a plumbing inspection, and finally for an overall construction inspection. Once the plumbing and electrical inspections are done, you can close the walls. When the construction is done, call your surveyor back to draw the new property lines. This is important for resale value. The addition becomes part of the new survey of your property, and for that you need a certificate of occupancy. Your property most likely will also be reassessed, and that assesment will affect your property taxes. A survey is the first thing I ask to see when I buy a house, and I expect to see the house exactly as it is on the survey.

How can I ensure that things run smoothly on the job?

Remember that the group of men and women who are working for you are employees with special skills who deserve respect. If your workers are doing a great job, it's worth coddling them a little. Bring them coffee, bagels, and muffins. Pay them on time. Cultivate a relationship with them. They will be happier and willingly help you with work in the future. And if you plan on buying other properties and developing them, it is important to have dependable people at your disposal. If some of the people you hire do not work out, try to replace them on the current job and do not hire them again. No-shows and sloppy workers cost you time and money and are unacceptable. Be frank and polite with less-than-satisfactory workers.

———— ! ————

Now that you have a grip on the overall way your home works, function by function, it's time to get down to the details. That means taking a look at your house room by room. The next section tackles all the ways you can upgrade, update, and personalize individual spaces in your home. Here's your chance to forever banish crummy kitchens, banal bathrooms, and lackluster landscaping (along with boring bedrooms and unfriendly family rooms) from your home and your life. What are you waiting for? Let's get started!

PART 3

ROOM-BY-ROOM IMPROVEMENTS

There are dozens of ways to enhance each room in your home. But where do you begin? When deciding what room to tackle first, consider what rooms you spend the most time in and which areas need the most attention. Is the baby blue tub/shower combo in your master bath giving you nightmares? Are any kitchen appliances or fixtures on their last legs? The kitchen and bathroom are good places to start because both rooms have to work so hard for us every day. It's no wonder, then, that improvements to these rooms also offer the most return for your investment, closely followed by outdoor improvements (and that's the order they'll be addressed in Part 3).

The finishes that you like the least in your new place should probably be changed first. If you dislike the family room paneling left over from the Brady Bunch era, maybe you should work on that first. What about your bedroom? Haven't you always wanted it to be a cozy, romantic retreat? Even though your home is an investment—and there's nothing wrong with money in the bank—the value of a home is also determined by the degree of enjoyment and comfort those living in it have. So in Part 3, I'll help you make decisions about personalizing your home for style and comfort, as well as for financial rewards.

Once you determine which projects make the most sense for your lifestyle, you'll need to determine your budget and plan accordingly. There's no sense in getting in over your head and quitting a project halfway through because you didn't anticipate some costs or timing issues.

So many rooms, so little time. It can be overwhelming, but not if you tackle one room at a time. Having multiple projects going on simultaneously in several (or even two) rooms, especially when you are living in the space, is challenging for you and your family. Completing one whole room before embarking on another project helps to keep your home life a little saner. So take one step at a time, put one foot in front of the other, and have fun!

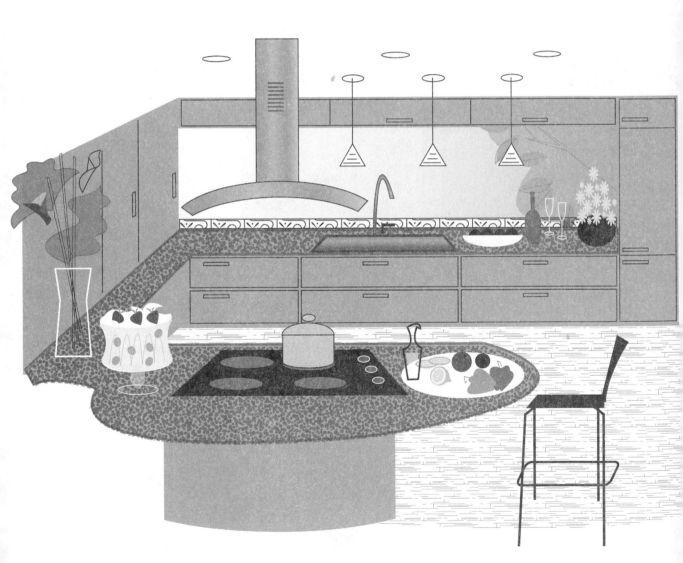

!

CHAPTER 6

The Crucial Kitchen

I don't know about you, but if my kitchen were my entry hall, the house would certainly stop there! Forget my beautiful living room, cozy TV room, or the amazing picture of Slash playing guitar in my workout room. My kitchen is a great space that I took special pride in when I was building the house. With all of my houses (past and present), I have always focused on the kitchen first. The appliances, countertops, cabinets, doors, archways, and windows have combined to make it a comfortable place for family and friends to hang out, talk, and feel cozy in. My son, Zachary, his friends, and my own friends always go right for our kitchen.

I think it's true for many people—the kitchen just ends up being the place where everyone congregates, even if you live on a steady diet of frozen and take-out food. I'm not a cook, but that did not stop me from building the best kitchen I could and making it look as if I can cook!

High functionality, visibility, and frequent use are what make a kitchen so valuable. It's one of the best rooms to put money into because it realizes the greatest return on investment in terms of both your own use and future resale value. You can see an 85 to 150 percent return on your investment with minor remodeling and 80 to 95 percent with major gut renovation, especially if you plan on selling within 2 or 3 years of the project's completion. In the meantime, you add so much to your life by having a modern, comfortable kitchen—no matter what its size and how humble your talents as a cook. It does not matter! A low-function kitchen drags a good house down in value, and a great kitchen can sell an otherwise modest house. Even a small condo benefits from a fantastic kitchen, especially at resale time. Up-to-date appliances and the latest fittings give your digs an edge over the competition.

KITCHEN REMODELING

The truth is that even a "minor" kitchen renovation can be a domestic nightmare. No matter how well planned it is or how capable the professionals involved are, tearing out a kitchen or even just replacing a worn countertop can become a disruption of theatrical proportions. Why bother to sugarcoat it? It's better to be prepared for the inconvenience before you begin than to be surprised in the middle, when you have no sink and only half of the cabinets have been delivered. Good advance planning does help, however. And just keep reminding yourself that the payoff is a beautiful new kitchen that will last a lot longer than that construction headache!

go to the pros

WORKING WITH A KITCHEN DESIGNER

If you want to paint the kitchen cabinets, change their hardware, install a kitchen backsplash, and call it a day, you can certainly take care of those improvements yourself. Tackling a complete kitchen face-lift, on the other hand, is a job for the pros.

Who does it?

So many different trades are involved in a kitchen makeover. Licensed professionals such as plumbers and electricians (whom we have already discussed) may have to do complicated rerouting of gas, plumbing, and electrical lines. Many other problems may have to be solved by experienced builders (see page 109 for important reminders about working with builders). Cabinets are also challenging to install, especially if your walls and floor aren't plumb and level. A carpenter knows how to measure, fit, adapt, shim, and shore cabinetry into less than perfect spaces. Because so many trades are involved in a kitchen renovation, I recommend that you hire a specialist in kitchen design if you are planning a full-scale change. Kitchen designers or architects have intimate knowledge of how kitchens function best as well as information about the latest products, materials, and appliances. Once you have a kitchen designer, you can supervise the tradespeople with the help of the designer and save money by not hiring a general contractor.

What should I look for in a kitchen designer?

Look for an independent Certified Kitchen Designer, or CKD. These professionals specialize in designing kitchens and are skilled at making the most of your available space and budget. They are also knowledgeable about the latest innovations in products and materials. In order to become a CKD, a designation administered by the National Kitchen and Bath Association, a designer must complete several years of training. A CKD designation is coveted in the industry, so requirements to earn them go far beyond space-planning ability and design talent. A certified designer has to understand building, construction, and mechanical and electrical systems. He or she has to know how to write specifications and draw plans that plumbers, electricians, and cabinet installers can interpret. They also have to be familiar with local building codes and safety and environmental regulations.

What does a kitchen designer do?

Working with a CKD is similar to working with an architect. He or she can simply draw up a plan based on your dreams, desires, and dollars and leave it at that, or continue working with all the tradespeople involved until the job is completed. In the initial meetings, your CKD will interview you at length to determine how you cook and live in the kitchen space. Now is the time to share all your ideas, notes, and pictures. Based on information from those meetings, the CKD sorts out priorities for the present and future. After that, the CKD will bring preliminary designs to review with you. Finally, the CKD submits a complete proposal setting out all of the work that is planned. The specifications should describe in detail all construction work, cabinetry, countertops, appliances, wiring, plumbing, and lighting, as well as the division of responsibilities for the work, a timeline, and an estimated budget detailing all charges.

How long does it take?

Depending on the size of your kitchen and the extent of the renovation, count on a minimum of 4 weeks to redo a galley-style kitchen in a condo and up to 12 weeks or longer for a big redo of a sprawling space.

How much will it cost?

While you can refresh surfaces and add new features for as little as $5,000, expect to pay anywhere from a *minimum* of $20,000 up to $100,000 and much more for a complete kitchen makeover (depending on finishes, appliances, stone, etc.). You can save money by getting some of the appliances and fixtures, such as sinks, faucets, lights, pot racks, and cabinet hardware, yourself.

What happens?

A lot! But before you do anything, you have to determine what your budget is. I don't think it's a bad idea to use the equity in your house to improve your kitchen. It is such a valuable, vital area of your home, why not do the best job you can?

Once you have determined a budget, the kitchen designer will help you design a layout. Bring some of your own ideas to the first meeting so he or she will know what you like. (Use the floor plan at the end of this chapter, on page 123, to get started.) Think about how you currently use your kitchen and what changes would make the arrangement of appliances and counters and the traffic flow work better. Make a list of all the things you love about your kitchen too, so that those highlights can be incorporated into the new design.

After you approve the remodeling plan, if it includes total gutting, the work crew will demolish the cabinets, remove the appliances, and ensure that all water and gas lines are securely shut off. The kitchen will be put back together in stages, usually from

$

barbara's best bet

USING YOUR EQUITY IN YOUR HOME TO IMPROVE IT

Once you close on a home and start making monthly payments on it, you are building equity. Equity is the difference between the market value of a property and the loan held against it. The opportunity to use equity to make your house worth even more (which increases your equity in it) is one of the benefits of home ownership. Home equity loans, also called second mortgage loans, are generally available for up to 85 percent of the appraised value of your home. Home equity loan payment schedules can range from 5 to 25 years (typically they run for 5, 10, or 15 years).

The qualifying process for a home equity loan is similar to that for a first mortgage (see page 5). Many banks say that to qualify for a home equity loan, you need two things: your credit must be in good standing and you have to document your income. Some lenders also offer home equity loans in the form of credit lines that let you obtain cash advances with a credit card or write checks for amounts up to a certain credit limit. There are no hard-and-fast rules on how much you can borrow against the value of your house. The amount of the loan can be based on how much you owe compared to the home's market value. Some lenders will give you a loan equal to a certain percentage of the market value of your home, and some will lend you more than 100 percent of its value if you have a small mortgage and good credit. I would be wary of taking out such a large loan, however, because if you default, the sale of your home may not cover what you owe.

the ground up. If plumbing, gas, or electrical lines have to be added or moved, that will be done first. New flooring will be laid and then the lower and upper cabinets will be installed. Templates will be made for countertops, and then they and the sinks will be installed, followed by appliances and light fixtures. Unforeseen structural problems or delays in the fabrication or delivery of any of these items can hold up the process, so it's a good rule of thumb to expect that a kitchen renovation will take a minimum of 25 percent longer than you initially think it will.

IMPROVISING A RENOVATION KITCHEN

If you plan to live in the house while the kitchen is being renovated (and few of us can afford to relocate while construction is under way), consider setting up an auxiliary kitchen. It can go a long way toward keeping your sanity intact. Plus, it's easy, efficient, and relatively inexpensive.

Select a location away from the dust and debris of the construction but still convenient and, if possible, near a sink. Set up a sturdy table (flimsy folding card tables are not recommended) to hold appliances, cutting boards, and basic cooking utensils. Cover the table with large heatproof mats or trivets, which are available at cooking supply stores. Gather the appliances* you think you will use the most:

- Mini refrigerator (place it on the floor next to the table; make sure the door is unobstructed and can open and close freely)

- Slow cooker

- Electric kettle

- Coffeemaker

- Toaster oven

- Microwave oven

- Electric coil cooktop (available as a single or double unit at kitchen specialty shops)

*For safety, always unplug small appliances when they are not in use.

CREATE A NEW FLOOR PLAN

If you're happy with the layout of your current kitchen, use that footprint to plan the placement of your cabinets and appliances. If you are not satisfied, analyze the way you use the kitchen now and create a new floor plan that will improve the workspace and general traffic patterns in the room. Consider tearing down a wall to create a great room or adding a wall for extra cabinet, countertop, and lighting space. Think about shifting appliances for a more efficient work triangle. A preliminary floor plan helps you think through what you really need and will be a valuable tool for the kitchen designer or cabinet consultant when he or she is developing the final plan. Spend at least a couple of hours assessing your kitchen and playing with a new design on paper. It may take a few tries to come up with something you really like that you can show to a kitchen designer.

Get started using the graph paper and worksheet templates on the following pages. Each box represents 6 inches. Measure your walls and draw the outline of your kitchen to include all of them. Mark door and window locations. If you want to relocate windows or doors, draw them in their new locations. If you are planning to add space, indicate that, too. Cut out or copy the appliance templates here and use standard cabinet measurements as a jumping-off point. Standard upper cabinets are 12 inches deep and 36 or 42 inches tall. Lower cabinets are 24 inches deep and 34 inches tall.

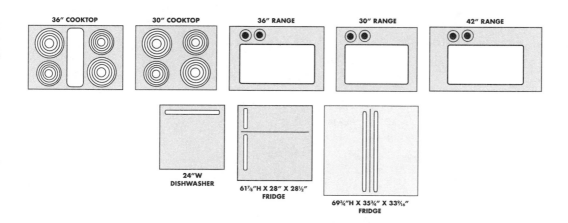

EACH SQUARE EQUALS 6 SQUARE INCHES

EACH SQUARE EQUALS 6 SQUARE INCHES

KITCHEN ASSESSMENT WORKSHEET

Use this worksheet to keep track of your kitchen project. It's a good place
to list brand names and prices of features you are considering.

ROOM DIMENSIONS: _____

CONDITION AND PROBLEMS: _____

_____

_____

_____

RENOVATION BUDGET:

MATERIALS	BRAND	DIMENSIONS	ITEM NUMBER/SKU	COST
SUB-FLOORING:				
FINISHED FLOORING:				
LIGHTING:				
WINDOWS:				
DOORS:				
WALL FINISHES:				
CABINETS:				
COUNTERTOPS:				
HARDWARE:				
SINK AND FAUCETS:				
APPLIANCES:				
			MATERIALS SUBTOTAL:	
LABOR				
PLUMBING:				
ELECTRICAL:				
HEATING:				
VENTILATION:				
CARPENTRY:				
OTHER:				
			LABOR SUBTOTAL:	
GRAND TOTAL:				

MATERIAL MATTERS

I don't think you should skimp on kitchen materials. Buy the best you can afford and spend money wisely by choosing items with high-quality construction, timeless design (think simple and elegant so you won't tire of them quickly), and high functionality. There's a lot to consider in a kitchen, so here's a brief look at everything you need to think about.

CABINETRY

New cabinets take up a big chunk of a construction budget. Before you replace them, make sure the old ones really have to go. If you hate the old, chipped laminate doors but the cabinet carcasses or boxes are sturdy and in good shape and you like their placement, they can be refaced and the doors replaced with any number of door styles at a fraction of the cost of entirely new cabinets. And it doesn't take much time, either. Cabinet refacing can be completed in a matter of days.

If the cabinets are wood, painting them a glossy white or other color and changing their hardware can make them look brand-new. It just takes a bit of elbow grease. If you are painting cabinets, it's best to empty them and remove the doors and hardware. Number the cabinet doors so you know where to reattach them. Cabinets should be thoroughly cleaned to remove grease and dirt, lightly sanded, primed, sanded again, and then given at least two coats of paint (sand lightly between coats) to get a hard, durable surface. You can also have the doors professionally spray-painted for between $10 and $20 per door.

If your cabinets are just too damaged, ugly, beyond repair, or inadequate, I think it's worth spending money on quality construction and materials. Cabinets are a kitchen's foundation—if you get them right, everything around them has a way of falling into place.

Demanding high-quality construction and high-end features does not mean you have to have cabinets custom-made. Manufacturers offer so many options now that you can achieve a custom look on a stock or semi-custom budget just by mixing things up a bit. Retailers who specialize in kitchen and bathroom design and cabinetry have good installers who know how to work with the materials. When they are well installed, standard cabinets look like a million bucks. Poorly installed cabinets, regardless of the cabinet sticker price, look cheap and shoddy.

In general, cabinets are separated into three categories: stock, semi-custom, and custom. Stock cabinets are straight off the rack (you can literally take some styles right from the shelves of big home improvement centers) and come in a somewhat limited range of styles, but they are the least costly of the three. Once ordered, they also come in very quickly, usually within a month. They start at around $100 per cabinet. If you go with stock cabinets, be sure to look for the Kitchen Cabinet Manufacturers Association certification sticker. It means that the cabinets have passed the same rigorous performance testing that higher-end cabinets are subjected to.

Semi-custom cabinets come in a wider range of styles and unusual sizes and are generally made with better materials than stock cabinets. They take a bit longer to arrive (up to 2 months after ordering) and cost more (starting at around $200 per cabinet) since they are made to order from a catalog of styles, colors, and materials. I bought some semi-custom unfinished cabinets with cutouts in the doors, then went to a glassmaker and really customized them with a special glass effect. They look ultracustom, but lacked the ultracustom price tag.

Custom cabinets are made to order by machine or hand by a cabinetmaker. They are based on your desires and exact measurements, which may not be the standard 24-inch-deep, 34-inch-tall base cabinet. They take the longest to arrive (up to 3 or 4 months in some cases) and cost the most. There is no limit to how much you can spend on custom cabinetry, but they start at $300 per cabinet.

You can get a very customized look by combining stock and semi-custom cabinets from the same manufacturer for a consistent look. Choose a mixture of doors (glass and solid, for instance) and heights and depths to achieve an individualized, custom look. For example, upper cabinets are usually 12 inches deep and 36 or 42 inches high. You can choose two different heights and stagger the cabinets for movement and variety. Or, you can forgo traditional upper cabinets and install a series of shelves instead. This modern, urban look is cost-effective because you can buy stock shelves in wood, which can be painted or stained, or stainless steel. Crown molding and trim are valuable add-ons that will elevate the status of a simple series of cabinets into an architectural feature (see page 73).

Don't stop at what cabinets look like on the outside. It's what's on the inside that really counts! Some stock and many semi-custom cabinets offer a variety of interior features, including knife drawers with inserts for holding blades securely, built-in spice racks, tray holders, pull-out pot and pan drawers, sliding breadboards, and drawers that shut slowly without slamming. Open shelves and basket storage have also gone from custom-only features to standard options.

Don't forget about cabinet "jewelry"—the hinges and pulls that help you open and close the drawers and doors. We often overlook them (who thinks about hinges?), but they are so important! Sturdy handles and easy-to-grab pulls are a must. Ask for fully adjustable hinges so doors can be brought back into line when they sag. The best hinges allow side-to-side, in-and-out, and up-and-down adjustment in addition to allowing doors to open wide. A snazzy upgrade for drawers is under-mount slides as opposed to side-mount slides. In either case, look for full extension slides so you can open drawers all the way.

COUNTERTOPS AND BACKSPLASH

Countertop and backsplash technology has come a long way in recent years. Here's what you need to know about the choices:

Natural stone is gorgeous and my favorite countertop material. I have white marble counters in my kitchen and marble counters and door saddles in the bathrooms in my house. Granite, limestone, slate, marble, and soapstone all have a very high-end look and certainly will add value to your home. Stone is also extremely heavy, durable, and resistant to heat. Granite and limestone are porous and need to be sealed periodically. They cost anywhere from $50 to $300 per linear foot installed, depending on the rarity of the color.

comfort zone

MAKING SPACE

Storage space: We all want it and never seem to have enough of it, especially in the kitchen. Use these tips to create space where there doesn't seem to be any:

- *Unused corners can be fitted with triangular shelves for holding jars.*

- *The space above and around the door is the perfect place for built-in shelves that can hold cookbooks and decorative china.*

- *Cup hooks screwed into the bottom of shelves can hold teacups and free up valuable shelf space.*

- *A rack secured to the ceiling can store pots and pans.*

Soapstone is extremely dense and only needs to be wiped with mineral oil every month or so. While it is heat resistant, cut marks will show and edges may chip if hit with pots and pans. You can cut drain gutters into and create sinks from soapstone for a totally integrated look. There's little choice of color or striations. The mineral oil brings out its natural coloring of black or dark gray with white veins. It costs $100 to $200 per linear foot installed.

Slate is nonporous and impervious to heat. Scratches can be rubbed out with steel wool. It costs from $70 to $200 per linear foot installed.

Marble stains easily but is beautiful in a kitchen. French, Italian, and Greek households, as well as many others around the world, have used marble for countertops for centuries, and European cooks consider its propensity to stain part of this material's inherent charm. It's also an excellent surface for rolling because it stays so cool. It costs from $60 to $150 per linear foot installed.

Engineered stone is a composite of quartz and resin. Because it combines a hard natural material with a strong resin, it is more scratch and stain resistant than solid surface materials. It looks like stone, but does not require periodic sealing. It has a modern look and comes in an array of colors. It can be cut to fit an under-mount sink, but a drain board cannot be cut into the surface. Depending on the brand, it can cost from $50 to $110 per linear foot installed.

Concrete is resistant to heat and scratches, but it is porous and prone to staining unless carefully sealed. But I do love this look. It can be mixed with any pigment for a vast array of colors. Fossils, glass, and even bits of jewelry can be imbedded in concrete for a truly personal counter style. Depending on the color, concrete can look industrial and modern or warm and soft. The cement used to make the concrete is inexpensive as a material, but the additives it needs for strength and the forms that need to be built for pouring it drive up the price. It costs from $75 to $150 per linear foot installed.

Wooden butcher block counters offer a natural look and are good for food preparation and overall durability, although they are not particularly heat resistant. Butcher block counters look awesome placed next to stone. I have seen kitchens with solid mahogany counters that are very beautiful—and very expensive. While scratches can be sanded out, butcher block and other wood counters need regular cleaning, and some woods need to be sealed to protect against bacteria. Butcher block costs from $50 to $75 per linear foot installed. Exotic solid hardwood counters can cost $100 and up per linear foot installed.

Solid surface (one brand name is Corian) is a seamless synthetic material, so it won't trap dirt. It is fairly stain and heat resistant and can be sanded and repaired if burned. Both countertop and sink can be made as one piece, and solid surface counters can also be cut and finished to accept an under-mount sink. Drain board gutters can be cut into the material. Some people—and I count myself among them—think solid surface material looks artificial; others feel it looks very urban and modern, particularly the solid colors (some styles have color flecks). It costs $60 to $110 per linear foot installed.

Ceramic or porcelain tile is more resistant to heat than solid surface materials, but it can crack and chip easily and requires regular maintenance to keep the grout

comfort zone

COUNTER TABLE

Countertop materials can be used for more than just topping off cabinets. Turn your kitchen table into a sturdy work surface by having a piece of counter material cut to fit on top of it. Solid and stone surfaces can be cut into virtually any shape, making them perfect for round, square, or oval tabletops and those with scalloped or other unusual corner styles and edges. Unifying the tabletop with your counters (using the same material but in a contrasting color) helps pull your kitchen's look together. Plus, the contrasting top highlights the shape of the table, bringing yet another architectural feature into your kitchen. Even better, a table surfaced with Corian or stone doubles as another work surface. However, the best part is that because these materials are heavy, they will stay in place without adhesives. Just make sure the table you are topping has sturdy legs and is structurally sound. The countertop fabricators will come to your house, make a template, and bring back and put in place the cut piece. Voilà! You'll have a fashionable, fabulous table that seamlessly coordinates with your kitchen counter.

clean and bacteria free. It comes in a huge array of colors and styles, so creativity is limitless. It costs from $10 to $45 per foot installed.

Laminate is the least expensive countertop you can buy. I don't recommend using it. While it comes in a large array of colors and patterns, it doesn't last long and is not sturdy. It's the least functional of all countertop materials. One other caveat: It cannot be cut for an under-mount sink installation. In general, laminates make a kitchen look dated, which certainly isn't appealing to today's home buyers. Recommended for quick, short-term fixes only! Laminates cost anywhere from $25 to $50 per linear foot installed.

—— on your own ——

Install a Tile Backsplash

Covering a plain drywall or laminate backsplash with tile is one way you can upgrade your kitchen yourself. This relatively simple and inexpensive project can add great value to your home. Tile adds sparkle, glitz, and richness to a kitchen. Plus, a backsplash is highly practical: Just wipe off splatters with a damp sponge!

How long will it take me? This is a great weekend project. Installation will take about a day. You must wait for the tile to set before grouting, which can be done the day after installation.

How much will it cost? It depends on what kind of tile you buy. Tile prices vary—stock 4 × 4-inch squares can be less than a dollar apiece. Handmade, glass, or marble tiles can cost several dollars per tile. You also need to buy supplies, which are not terribly expensive. You can tile your backsplash for as little as $300, or more if you want designer tiles.

What do I need? Tiling requires special, but inexpensive, equipment.

Tape measure

Glazed ceramic wall tiles (remember, buy 10 percent more than you need; see below for instructions on measuring your space)

Palm sander and coarse sandpaper if you are placing tile over laminate

Screwdriver

Rubber work gloves

Waterproof mastic tile adhesive

Notched trowel

Level

Plastic spacers sized for your tile

Sponge

Manual tile cutter

Tile nippers

Waterproof grout

Safety glasses

Damp cloth

Rubber grout float

Metal screws to replace existing switch-plate and outlet-cover screws, which will be too short once you apply the tile. Take the existing screws to the hardware store to find screws that match their width but are longer. The new screws should be $1\frac{1}{4}$ to $1\frac{5}{8}$ inches long.

Plastic washers

How do I do it?

1. First, check the mounting wall to ensure that it is dry and sturdy enough to hold the weight of the tiles. If you have damaged drywall, repair or replace it.

2. Decide how far up the wall the backsplash should extend. A back-splash can extend anywhere from 4 inches up from the countertop to all the way up to the underside of the cabinets. I think a backsplash that goes from countertop to cabinet bottom is the most desirable and luxurious. If you are doing it yourself, why not go all the way?

3. Measure the length and width of the backsplash area. If you have a

U-shaped or galley-style kitchen and plan to tile more than one wall, measure each wall individually. Determine the square footage by multiplying the length by the width of each wall you are covering. If applicable, add all the figures to get an overall total. You buy tile in square-foot quantities, so take this number with you to the store. Add 10 percent more to the total so you have extra tiles in case of breakage and extra cuts. Save leftover tiles in case damage occurs later on.

4. Select a tile you love that blends with the existing finishes in your kitchen (or that will go well with finishes you plan to add later). Ceramic tiles come in many colors and styles—square, mosaic set on mesh, brick-shaped. Have fun, but take care when selecting something extremely specific—you may tire of it more quickly than you would of a tile with classic color and style.

5. If you have laminate paneling covering the backsplash, tile adhesives will not stick to it and the tiles eventually will fall off. An easy solution is to sand the laminate with the coarsest sandpaper you can find to create a "tooth" for the adhesive to hold on to. Laminate is tough stuff, so only the coarsest sandpaper roughens the surface enough to proceed with the tiling. Use the palm sander in a circular motion to quickly sand the large parts of the backsplash, then sand by hand in smaller areas, around windows, and in tight corners. You could sand the whole area by hand, but it would take longer. If your backsplash is a painted surface, simply clean it and let it dry, then sand lightly with medium-grit sandpaper. Clean off any dust before proceeding.

6. Clear countertops of all small appliances and turn off the power to the electrical outlets in the area where you are working. Remove the electrical outlet covers and switch plates. Clean the area with a household sponge and warm water. Allow it to dry.

7. If you have a tiled countertop, plan the layout so the backsplash's grout veins line up with the countertop's grout veins. You can use the countertop tiles as a guide. If you don't have a tiled countertop, start by centering the first tile at the bottom of the backsplash. Use a tape measure to find the center and mark it lightly with a pencil.

8. Put on a pair of rubber or latex gloves. Apply the adhesive the tile manufacturer recommended with a notched trowel by holding the tool at a 45-degree angle and spreading a thin (about $\frac{1}{16}$-inch-thick) layer on the wall. Work in 3×3-foot areas so the adhesive doesn't dry out.

9. Lay the first tile in the center along the bottom of the backsplash so any odd cuts needed to make the tiles fit are at either end, where they will be less noticeable. Position the tile using a gentle twisting motion so it settles into the adhesive. Use a level to make sure the tile is square. Place a spacer at each corner of the first tile. Cut off one end of the spacers so they fit between the countertop and the bottom of the tile. Push the spacers into the adhesive.

10. Working outward from the first tile, continue laying the tiles in a row, flush against the spacers. Use a sponge to wipe off adhesive that oozes up between the tiles. Place spacers at the corners of each tile as you go to maintain even spacing. Check occasionally to make sure the tiles are level. After one row is complete, begin with the next row and follow the same adhesive, tile, and spacer application routine until you are done.

11. If you need to cut a tile to fit at the end of the row, score the tile with a tile cutter. Follow the manufacturer's instructions for using the tile nippers or tile cutter to remove the scored area. When placing tiles around outlets, make sure that the outlet cover will overlap the tile edges when it is reinstalled.

12. When you have laid all the tiles, wipe off any excess adhesive with a damp cloth. Keep rinsing the cloth and wiping the tile until all of the excess adhesive has been removed from the surface of the tiles.

13. Consult the adhesive manufacturer's instructions to determine how long it takes the adhesive to set. After the adhesive sets, remove all the spacers.

14. Mix the grout according to the manufacturer's instructions. Grout is irritating to the skin and eyes, so you must wear safety glasses when mixing it and rubber or latex gloves when working with it.

15. Apply the grout using a rubber grout float. Spread the grout diagonally at a 45-degree angle across the tiles, packing the grout between the tiles by using gentle pressure. Wipe off the excess grout with a damp sponge when the grout becomes firm, but not dry.

16. Clean the tiles again and smooth the grout with a damp sponge.

17. After the grout dries a haze will be visible. Wipe off the tiles and polish them with a clean cloth.

18. Replace the electrical outlet covers and switch plates. You will need longer screws. Use 1¼- to 1⅝-inch-long screws and place plastic washers behind the screws securing the outlet or switch to the wall to bring it flush with the tile.

19. Make yourself a cup of tea, sit back, and enjoy your fabulous new backsplash!

SINKS AND FAUCETS

Sinks come in a variety of finishes and materials, from stone and stainless steel to porcelain and solid surface. What you choose depends on the style of your kitchen. Here's what to consider:

Size. The dimensions of your sink are determined by the size of the base cabinet it will be installed in. Thirty-six-inch-wide, 10-inch-deep sinks let you soak dishes, pots, and pans after a dinner party or even bathe a small child or the family pug. Small, round bowls are great as second utility sinks placed in an island or in another countertop adjacent to the main sink.

Number of bowls. Sinks now come in many bowl configurations, including two bowls of equal size, one large bowl and a smaller bowl, and two large bowls and a smaller tub. Think about how you use your current sink and what features would make it more functional.

Mount style. Under-mount sinks are installed below the edge of the countertop with metal clips. Over-mount sinks have a lip that overlaps the edge of the countertop. Over-mount sinks are generally less expensive than the under-mount style, but under-mount sinks are more sanitary and easier to keep clean. I love mine. Food and other kitchen waste can be pushed from the countertop into the sink without anything getting trapped between the lip of the sink and the countertop. No caulk is applied between the lip of the sink and the countertop, and water will not seep through the crevice and damage the countertop. The cutout for the sink is more complicated—it needs to be perfectly finished. Add to the sink's depth the thickness of the countertop to make sure the sink will fit in your cabinet. A 10-inch-deep sink becomes an 11- or 12-inch-deep sink when under-mounted in stone or quartz. Under-mount sinks are more desirable in high-end kitchens, so keep that in mind if you are planning to sell soon.

Kitchen faucets add function and a bit of sparkle to the sink area, and nowadays faucets come in a huge array of styles, finishes, and price points (from $50 at the lowest end to more than $1,000 at the highest end). Here's what you need to consider:

Style. Faucets can be as minimal or elaborate as you like. Integrated models with sprayers that pull out from a single spout are simple and modern. Double-handled faucets with a center spout are more traditional.

Finishes. Chrome, stainless steel, nickel, aged copper, forged iron, and brushed metal finishes—the list is endless. Special finishes cost more, so keep that in mind when you're making your selection. You also might tire of a unique finish that dates quickly. Highly specific finishes and colors also don't appeal to a wide range of buyers. Yet faucets are for the most part affordable and easily changed, so you can indulge in a finish you really love and change it later if you get bored with it.

Accessories. Sprayers, integrated soap dispensers, and built-in water filters are just some of the accessories you can choose as part of your faucet assembly.

APPLIANCES

A large side-by-side refrigerator, a six-burner stainless steel gas range with a convection oven, and a superquiet dishwasher offer a lot of functionality, especially in a busy kitchen that doubles as a dining and entertaining center. If you are an avid cook, you may want to consider upgrading to professional kitchen equipment. If so, be prepared to pay up to three times as much for professional appliances than you would for residential-grade standard appliances. Professional-grade equipment designed for home use is made of supersturdy materials and can take a lot of wear and tear. Plus, great appliances are good for resale—people sometimes choose a house based on its excellent appliances!

Before spending big bucks on appliances, take the time to research and understand your housing market—appliances, especially the high-end brands, are expensive. If you live in a place like Manhattan, Miami, or Los Angeles, top-drawer appliances are a must in residential redos. But if you live in a less-glitzy city or suburb, the $1,000 fridge (as opposed to the $3,500 one) or $1,500 range (instead of the $5,000 version) might be just as good for your own use and for resale. If you're on a limited budget, other items, such as wood floors or new windows, might be more desirable and practical for your lifestyle than "designer" appliances.

Appliance decisions should be based on not only your budget, but also your intentions. What purpose will your kitchen serve? Do you want it to impress your friends and neighbors? Do you want it to help you create simple, nutritious meals for your family? Do you want it to be Entertainment Central and provide space for parties, or do you want to practice your gourmet cooking—or all four? Each of these reasons is legitimate. Determine what you want your kitchen to be to help you select the right appliances. For example, if your aim is to have an impressive kitchen and money is no object, then by all means buy the latest, most high-tech appliances available. Or, if you are a gourmet chef who wants the best, brand names such as Sub-Zero, Wolf, Garland, Thermador, and Viking should be music to your ears.

Yet you can still create a fantastic meal—and a beautiful kitchen—with mid-range appliances, whether you are a budding culinary master on a limited budget or someone who wants a kitchen only for storing champagne and diet soda. That's especially true today, when so many appliance manufacturers are adding high-end features to midlevel appliances, including "library quiet" motors and insulation in refrigerators and dishwashers and high-Btu flames and simmer settings on cooktops. Regardless of how much money you decide to spend on appliances, here's a checklist of items and features that are must-haves. The good news is that they are available at almost every price level:

Refrigerator/freezer. Side-by-side or freezer-on-the-bottom styles; ice maker; quiet motor; temperature zones for keeping a variety of foods fresh at individually set temperatures

Dishwasher. Superquiet models with ample insulation; stainless steel interiors; adjustable racks for tall, long, and oddly shaped items

Range. Burners with multiple Btu levels, from high to a gentle simmer (a Btu, or British thermal unit, is the quantity of heat needed to increase the temperature of 1 pound of water by 1 degree Fahrenheit from a specified temperature); dual conventional and convection ovens; dual fuel (gas for the cooktop, electricity for the oven). For wall ovens, doors that open sideways make it easy to get food in and out. For cooktops, five or six burners are better than four (if you have space).

Venting system. Range vents that vent to the outside instead of recirculating the air are best, although it may not be possible to install them in some apartments and houses, depending on how difficult it is to access the outside; hidden systems, which appear and disappear behind the cooktop with the touch of a finger

Microwave oven. Models that double as oven vents; dual-function microwaves that can also be used as convection ovens; large-capacity microwaves

comfort zone

LASTING FINISHES

Keep in mind that the latest design trends are expensive and may not have lasting value. The red stove, glass sink, or checkerboard mahogany floor may look very stylish now, but could look outdated in just a few years. The extra dollars you shell out for such items won't pay you back when it's time to sell. Neutral colors (white, black, and stainless for appliances, for example) and classic silhouettes (think wide-plank floors with no decorative inset pattern and plain white pedestal bathroom sinks) stand the test of time. You can change the décor by changing the accessories that surround the basics for a look that's always fresh.

FLOORING

Kitchen flooring runs the gamut from vinyl sheet flooring or tiles, to hardwood, to ceramic and stone tile. I like the beach-house style of the painted wood floor in my kitchen. It's also easy to clean, and the finish is supertough. But wood floors also have to be protected in heavy-use areas, such as in front of the stove and sink. Even then, you may notice some wear over the years. On the other hand, I have yet to have a problem with mine, and when I get the chance in a new place, I'll use wood again.

Ceramic tile is the most popular choice for kitchens. It's durable and easy to clean. You can find ceramic tile in a wide price range, so it's very affordable. The labor involved in laying tile is where the expense lies. It's not that difficult to lay a tile floor yourself, though. Ceramic tiles can cost anywhere from $2 to $50 per square foot, depending on the style. Installation can run anywhere from $2.50 to $8 or more per square foot depending on the intricacy of the design you want and the region you live in. Consider combining an inexpensive field tile with more expensive decorative borders, medallions, or inserts. A *field tile* is a basic tile, like a white subway-style tile, that covers the greatest area and is punctuated with a more expensive tile material (such as marble or granite) or decorative handmade or hand-painted tiles.

Stone is also a popular choice, but it is more expensive than ceramic tile. Limestone, granite, and marble are all beautiful flooring options. A professional should install stone floors (see "Go to the Pros: Install a Stone Floor," page 68). Expect to pay from $15 to $60 per square foot. Installation can also be pricey because stone is heavy and hard to cut; expect to pay from $5 to $20 a square foot to install.

Slate is a good choice for kitchens, but it is porous and should be sealed to protect it from staining. Slate is typically mined in India and parts of Asia where it is plentiful (and labor is cheap), so even with freight to the United States it is still very affordable and can often be found for less than $5 a square foot. Installation runs between $2.50 and $20 per square foot, and prices vary by region.

Concrete is a great option if you're going for a contemporary, industrial look. It must be sealed and has a tendency to crack, which many people feel is part of its beauty and character. The labor required in pouring, smoothing, polishing, and sealing a concrete floor drives up the price, which can run up to $30 per square foot to install.

Terra-cotta and brick are also beautiful kitchen floor options—they have a rustic look that works for country-style kitchens and as a brilliant contrast against modern finishes like stainless steel appliances. Both are porous and need sealing, but the material itself is affordable. Expect to pay between $3 and $10 a square foot to buy, and about $2.50 to $5 per square foot to install. Prices vary by region.

Cork is a natural material (cork oak tree bark) that is easy to care for, durable, and very comfortable to stand on for long periods, making it a good choice for a busy cook. It must be sealed after installation due to its porosity. Cork is affordable, too—cork tiles cost about $2.50 to $5 a square foot and about the same to install, including sealing. If you are ambitious, you can install cork tiles yourself. You can also buy cork in sheets, but installation would not be a do-it-yourself project. However, the cost is about the same. One of the reasons cork has come down in price so much is that it is being fabricated into flooring by a variety of manufacturers and the quality is not always up to par. Buy cork flooring from a reputable dealer and make sure it comes with a warrantee.

Bamboo is a sustainable natural product that used to be a high-end material and now has come down in price quite a bit. You can find it for anywhere from $3 to $8 per square foot. It installs

comfort zone

A LUXURIOUS KITCHEN

It's your house and you should buy what you love. Chances are that someone else is going to love it, too. The luxury details are often what people fall in love with. For instance, if you really love wine, why not add a wine fridge to the kitchen? If you have a passion for soup or pasta, install a pot filler by your stove (this involves running a water line to the stove area, which may be far from the sink). A built-in marble surface is handy for rolling out pastry, a wooden cutting surface that is set into the countertop but removable for easy cleanup makes cutting and chopping veggies and fruits a snap, and an under-the-counter beverage center that includes a turbocharged ice maker and room for sodas is perfect for entertaining. A walk-in pantry and laundry center are convenient, especially if you have children. If you are crazy for coffee, a built-in cappuccino and espresso maker might make getting up for work a little easier!

like a wood floor and costs the same—about $2.50 to $2.75 per square foot. The price of bamboo has fallen recently because of its popularity and the growing number of producers. Because of this market growth the material's quality varies widely. Make sure the bamboo you are buying comes from the middle of the bamboo stalk (the material taken from the top and bottom is not as strong), was at least 6 years old when it was harvested (younger bamboo is softer), and is in its natural color, because the process used to create darker browns weakens the material. Let the bamboo acclimate to your environment for about a week before installing. Also note that bamboo darkens very slightly over time as it is exposed to sunlight.

Vinyl is the least expensive choice for kitchen flooring, but I also think it is the least desirable. It wears out quickly and, depending on the texture, can be hard to clean (dirt that gets stuck in any grooves can be nearly impossible to get out). Manufacturers are getting better at producing vinyl products that look like ceramic and stone. As a short-term solution, vinyl might be the way to go, but I don't recommend it. If you must use it, expect to pay from $5 to $10 per square foot.

on your own

Create a Kitchen Island

Islands are favorite features in any kitchen. You can create your own custom island from a bureau purchased at an unfinished furniture store or, for even more character, an antique or secondhand shop. When painted or stained a contrasting color, this unique island makes a personal statement—and the trend now is toward making built-in islands look more like pieces of furniture. Why not use the real thing? The drawers are perfect for storing all sorts of kitchen equipment and pantry items. Backing it with pegboard creates even more space for hanging small utensils. Or, back it with bead board for a decorative finish.

Top your creation with the same material you used on your countertops for a unified look and a practical workspace. Or, find an old piece of marble or other stone at an architectural salvage shop for more one-of-a-kind charm. No one else will have an island quite like yours, and the good news is that you can either take it with you when you move or leave it for the next inhabitants to enjoy. Gorgeous personality pieces overflowing with charm sometimes cinch sales! Just make sure you state clearly what goes with you and what sells with the house.

How long will it take me? Several hours—how about reserving a weekend afternoon?

How much will it cost? A bureau from an unfinished furniture store can cost a few hundred dollars; a sturdy example from an antique or secondhand shop could cost as little as $50. Paint and supplies are of minimal cost (if you don't already have them). Prices vary widely for countertops, depending on what kind you install. If you shop wisely, you can have yourself a kitchen island for well under $500—compared to several thousand for a ready-made version. Plus, you'll know you did it yourself!

What do I need? The most important element is the bureau itself. Measure your space to find just the right size. Unfinished furniture stores can build one to your dimensions for a very reasonable price. If your heart is set on a vintage piece, it may take you more time to find just the right fit. In addition to the bureau, you need:

Tape measure

A countertop cut to size by the countertop supplier; a vintage marble top can be cut at a stone yard

Four to six 6-, 8-, or 10-inch legs from a home improvement store, depending on the length and height of your bureau

Paint or stain: Water-based primer is adequate. A kitchen- or bath-grade water-based paint in a gloss finish will be easy to clean. Because you are topping off the island with countertop material, painting the top is not essential.

Application materials, including brushes and paper towels or clean rags for applying stains

Pegboard or bead-board paneling from a home improvement center (optional)

Saw

Wood glue

Finishing nails

Hammer

Fine-grit sandpaper

Power drill

How do I do it?

1. Measure the space where you want to place the island. Make sure you leave about 2½ to 3 feet from the perimeter of the nearest counter for easy traffic flow.

2. Measure the top of the bureau and order a countertop for it in any material you like. You can match it to your existing countertops or find another material that coordinates.

3. If you are ordering the bureau from a store that makes unfinished furniture, ask them to make it in the width and depth you want and 35 inches high. A 1-inch-thick countertop will then make it a 36-inch-high island, which is a standard height for kitchen counters.

4. Vintage bureaus are usually 31 to 32 inches high, including the existing legs. The bureau itself, without the legs, could be 28 inches high, for example. That means you have to buy 6- or 8-inch-high legs to bring it up to the right height. The countertop will add at least another inch in height. If the bureau is longer than 45 inches, you'll need six legs to create a stable base, with the extra two placed at the center of each long side.

5. Once you have the bureau and legs, examine the back. A new piece from an unfinished furniture store might have a plain or luaun plywood back that can be easily painted or stained. An older piece might not have such an attractive back. Either way, consider applying an inexpensive piece of bead-board or pegboard paneling. The sheets come in 4 × 8-foot pieces and are easy to cut with a standard wood saw. Measure the back and cut the piece to size, then attach it with wood glue and finishing nails. Sand the edges smooth with fine-grit sandpaper.

6. If you are using an old bureau, take off the existing legs (normally they screw off, but if they do not, cut them off with your wood saw). Screw in the new legs using the existing holes or drill holes if you had to saw off the legs. The bureau should reach a height of at least 33 or 34 inches, but ideally it will be 35 or 36 inches high. Remember that the countertop will add an inch or so, and the island does not have to match the height of your other counters.

7. Next, paint or stain the piece (and the legs, if necessary). If you are painting an old piece, be sure to sand it lightly and clean it thoroughly first.

8. Position your new kitchen island now, before you top it with the counter material. Otherwise, it will be too heavy to lift. Position the countertop on the top and voilà! You have got yourself a kitchen island!

———— ❗ ————

Once you've got the kitchen covered, getting your bathroom in the best possible shape will improve your quality of life and add tremendous value to your home, as well. In the next chapter I will review all your options—and tell you what features are worth paying for and which ones are best left on the showroom floor.

!

CHAPTER 7

The Indispensable Bathroom

I always say you can never lose by spending money on bathrooms because you can never have too many! Like most home buyers, after the kitchen, I believe that bathrooms are the next most important features of a house. I *always* add more bathrooms if there aren't enough (one for every bedroom) when I buy a new home. If there are enough but they aren't up to the standard, I am quick to start calculating a renovation budget! From limestone to glass, from wall borders to lighting, from windows to great glass doors for the shower, there is no end to what you can use to create your perfect bathroom.

So much time is spent in bathrooms, why not make them perfect for your home and your lifestyle? For example, my master bath has marble countertops and a marble tub surround, limestone walls and floors, a luxurious shower, ample robe hooks, heated towel bars, and a big picture window, all of which lend it the air of a four-star spa at an ocean retreat (and that's exactly how I think of my house at the beach). Yet the finishes and materials I used also make it very functional for days when I have to get out the

147

door for work or when I'm rushing to get ready for a date. Even the more modestly sized and simply styled bathrooms in my house have beautiful finishes and features. That makes them comfortable and relaxing for my family and guests.

You can add on or renovate a bathroom (or two) with relative ease and less inconvenience than a kitchen redo. Even a smallish bathroom in a condo can be expanded if there's a closet nearby. At the very least, it can be updated to include the latest cabinetry and fixtures. Don't underestimate the power of the powder room: A good bathroom renovation offers a 70 percent return on your investment; if it's a top-to-bottom redo of an out-of-date bath, you could realize a 100 percent or more return, because a new bathroom gives the impression the whole house has been renovated.

The bathroom, like the kitchen, is a room in which form follows function, so pay close attention to the details. That's as true for homes with a small bathroom with a shower/tub combination as it is for homes with a large, luxurious spalike bathroom with a separate shower and tub, a double sink, a marble floor, and a dressing area. A bathroom should work for you, not against you.

On the other hand, a bathroom designed solely around function ignores two very important elements: comfort and relaxation. In the morning, when I am getting ready for work or my son, Zachary, is rushing to get ready for school, expediency is paramount. But after work or on the weekend, I want to luxuriate in the tub or take a very long, very hot shower. My bathroom has to offer both convenience and atmosphere. Doesn't everyone want that? A bathroom redo must take into account who will be using the bathroom, when, and for what purpose.

BATHROOM REMODELING

To renovate or add a bathroom, you can be sure that you will have to contact plumbing, electrical, carpentry, tiling, and HVAC experts. You can contract the job yourself (see "Be Your Own Project Manager," page 90). You'll also need to hire a contractor who specializes in bathroom renovation and building or a professional kitchen and bath designer to help you determine the best use of space. If you are adding a bathroom extension to your house, an architect specializing in additions can show you the best ways to extend off of an existing room. See Chapter 5 for tips on working with architects.

Depending on the details and finishes you choose and the size of the bathroom, a surface face-lift (new sink or vanity, faucet, and flooring) can be done for as little as $2,500 or less if you do some of the work yourself, like replacing the faucet or installing the floor. A total gutting can cost as much as $30,000 and much, much more. Whatever level of renovation you choose, when it comes to bathroom upgrades, throwing money *into* the drain (and the shower, flooring, lighting, and cabinets) is a wise investment!

ASSESS YOUR SPACE

Before a hammer hits the wall, the first thing a contractor or kitchen and bath designer does is look at what you've got so the two of you can decide where you can go. Assessing your bathroom is the first step in making smart changes.

Ventilation

Older bathrooms often have inadequate ventilation systems. Replace noisy, inefficient bathroom fans with modern, quiet versions. Make sure they vent to the outside. If your bathroom doesn't have a fan, install one.

Plumbing and electric

It's a good idea to have a plumber and electrician help you evaluate what you've got (and what you're missing). Here's what to consider:

- Is the electrical service adequate for the number of outlets and circuits required and for future expansion? If not, plan on adding outlets on both sides of vanities or sinks. Equip outlets around sinks with ground-fault circuit interrupters to prevent shocks (see page 50 for more information on GFCIs).

- Does the existing plumbing work well? Is there adequate water pressure? Do the drains flow quickly? Check out Chapter 3 for how to deal with low pressure (page 54).

- Are there any leaks or is there evidence of water damage near or around pipes? Fix or replace them right away. Leaky pipes will damage new materials.

- Are any pipes made from lead or galvanized steel (both common in houses built before 1950)? If so, replace them. Lead piping and corroded metals might contaminate the water and eventually cause other problems like clogs, cracks, and breaks. You don't want to deal with that!

CONSIDER YOUR LIGHTING

Have you ever considered how much time you actually spend in the bathroom? If I had a dollar for every time I went to primp for a date in front of my bathroom mirror . . . That's one reason it's so important to have great lighting in a bathroom—bad lighting can turn good makeup into a bad date! The bathroom is where you prepare to look your best, and good lighting is key, from the number of fixtures and where you place them to what kind of lightbulb you choose. Have you ever tried on a bathing suit in a dressing room with dim fluorescent lighting? Who looks good in that light? Yuck! Put some thought and money into your bathroom lighting—everyone who uses the space will be amazed by how the right light changes the whole room (and how they feel about themselves).

I love a bathroom that has a variety of light sources, including a central ceiling fixture for general lighting (install a dimmer switch to make bath time more relaxing), sconces flanking or above the main mirror, and a flush-to-the-ceiling fixture over the shower. Consider using blue bulbs that simulate natural light instead of harsh white bulbs.

BATHROOM FIXTURES

Fixtures need to suit your personal needs and lifestyle. If you love to escape to your bathroom at the end of a long day, upgrades like a Swiss shower (which has multiple showerheads that hit you from all directions), a rain shower, or a deep soaking tub give you a little vacation retreat right down the hall. I love these features, especially in a master bathroom, and so do a lot of other people, making them worthy investments:

- A spacious shower with multiple heads enclosed by a thick, seamless glass door and a built-in seat or bench

- A solid piece of stone is so much easier to clean than a tile countertop—grout lines that get infected with dirt and mold are tough to keep up with.

- A double sink set into a stone-topped vanity. A vessel sink makes a ho-hum bathroom look like part of an upscale hotel suite.

- Ceramic or stone tile floors are easy to care for and look rich. Be sure to select a tile with a matte or pebbled texture for safety. Smooth surfaces are slippery when wet.

- A linen closet gives you a discreet storage option. If you can't fit a closet into the room because of structural or budget issues but you have the space for it, add an armoire with shelves.

CREATE A NEW FLOOR PLAN

Make a list of everything you want in your bathroom—including the items you think are out of reach. You can find a way to add them if you really want them when you are done planning your bathroom. First, measure your walls and draw the outline of your bathroom, including all the walls, on the graph paper provided on page 152. Each box represents 6 inches. Mark door and window locations (including windows and skylights). If you want to relocate windows or doors, draw them in their new locations. If you plan to add space, indicate that, too. Cut out or copy the vanity, pedestal sink, tub, shower, and toilet templates below for easy placement. Have fun!

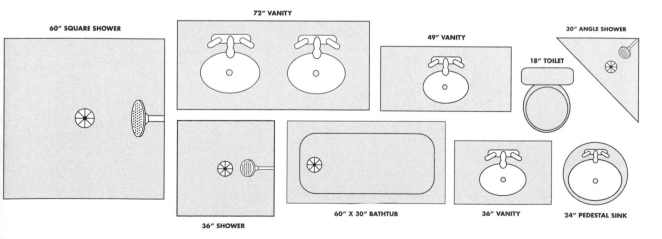

60" SQUARE SHOWER

72" VANITY

49" VANITY

30" ANGLE SHOWER

18" TOILET

36" SHOWER

60" X 30" BATHTUB

36" VANITY

24" PEDESTAL SINK

EACH SQUARE EQUALS 6 SQUARE INCHES

EACH SQUARE EQUALS 6 SQUARE INCHES

BATHROOM ASSESSMENT WORKSHEET

Use this worksheet to keep track of your bathroom project. It's a good place
to list brand names and prices of features you are considering.

ROOM DIMENSIONS:

CONDITION AND PROBLEMS:

RENOVATION BUDGET:

MATERIALS	BRAND	DIMENSIONS	ITEM NUMBER/SKU	COST
SUB-FLOORING:				
FINISHED FLOORING:				
LIGHTING:				
WINDOWS/SKYLIGHTS:				
DOORS:				
CABINETS:				
COUNTERTOPS:				
HARDWARE:				
SINK AND FAUCETS:				
BATH:				
SHOWER:				
FIXTURES:				
WALL FINISHES:				
			MATERIALS SUBTOTAL:	
LABOR				
PLUMBING:				
ELECTRICAL:				
HEATING:				
VENTILATION:				
CARPENTRY:				
OTHER:				
			LABOR SUBTOTAL:	
GRAND TOTAL:				

comfort zone

SPA LUXURY AT HOME

There are so many fantastic extras that you can add to your home bathroom nowadays—fixtures that once were available only to high-end spas and a few lucky home owners with access to designers and fancy showrooms. Now, many "luxury" features are on the market at every price level. Making your bathroom the special get-away-from-it-all room that it should be is within your reach! Here are some of my favorite over-the-top extras:

- *A heated floor is the ultimate luxury. Standing on a cold floor to brush your teeth does not give you a bright start on a busy day. Some radiant heating systems can be installed before new flooring goes in (see page 57 for details).*

- *Heated towel bars warm towels and dry clothes, and some units even double as radiators to heat the room. Most units are imported from Europe or Canada and can be pricey.*

- *A magnifying mirror and makeup lights. Great hotel luxury right at home!*

- *A sunken or whirlpool bathtub. Great for long soaks to wash away the cares of the day.*

- *Thermostatic shower valves precisely control the temperature of the water—you'll never step into a too-cold or too-hot shower again!*

- *Multiple showerheads provide a deluxe wake-up call.*

- *A walled-off toilet; even a half-wall offers privacy for busy couples who share a master bath. If you have enough space to add a room for the toilet within the bathroom, that's even better.*

- *Phone lines, intercom speakers, audio speakers, televisions, and even water-proof laptops are available to make your bathing experience more pleasant or productive.*

THE BATHROOM SINK

A quality sink and faucet are essential when it comes to bathroom comfort, style, and value. There's no excuse for ignoring a rusty, chipped, or stained sink. Upgrading a bathroom sink is easy and inexpensive, whether you do it yourself or hire a professional. A new sink doesn't have to cost much, and it can change the whole appearance and even the function of your bathroom. Here are your options:

Number of bowls. For busy couples on the same schedule, a double sink is a must in master bathrooms. If you have children, installing a double sink in their bathroom is not a bad idea either—especially if they are teenagers who spend more time styling their hair than doing their homework.

Mount style. Bathroom sinks come in a variety of mount styles: over-mount, under-mount, and top-mount. An over-mount sink is the most common and the easiest to install because it does not require a precise cut in the vanity top. An under-mount sink must be mounted precisely, so the cutout for it has to be exact. Top-mounted sinks, which are stylish these days, look like bowls sitting on the counter. Some top-mounted sinks have a platform that holds a special faucet designed specifically for use with vessel sinks. Others are simple bowls with one drain hole and the faucet installed into the countertop of the vanity. Some vessel sinks have overflow drains (the little hole at the top of the sink to catch overflowing water) and some do not. Those that do require special piping to attach the hole to the wastewater system. If you choose one that does not have an overflow hole, you have to be careful not to let the water run over when the drain is closed, so it may not be an ideal choice for a house with children.

Materials. The standard bathroom sink is an under-mounted porcelain or enameled cast-iron style. Also the most affordable, they are quite durable. You can also find glass (which can be hard to keep clean), stainless steel (which looks modern but somewhat institutional), and stone sinks. These three materials raise the price of the sink.

Faucet finishes and styles. Bathroom faucets, like kitchen faucets, come in many finishes, from chrome to stainless steel to gold-plated brass to brushed nickel. Porcelain or wooden handles add a vintage flair to modern, efficient faucets. The finish you choose should match the bathroom. Don't feel that all the faucets have to be consistent throughout a house unless you like that look. Each faucet can suit each bathroom's style and décor. As for styles—there are so many. Single-handle faucets give you warm water with a flick of your wrist, while separate hot and cold faucets are more traditional. Faucets with a wide, flat spout provide a waterfall effect that's very modern (and expensive). As I mentioned above, faucets made for vessel sinks are unique-looking, but they work the same way as conventional faucets. Countertop- or sink-mounted styles are usually taller than conventional faucets, but they don't require any special installation. Wall-mounted styles have a long spout that extends over the sink so the water falls from farther above.

on your own

Install a New Top-Mount Faucet

If your bathroom is basically in good shape, you can spruce it up with some new towel bars, thick, fluffy towels, and accessories like bars of scented soap and jars of oils and bath salts. Take those easy-to-find refreshers to the next level by adding a shiny new faucet. Don't call a plumber: You can switch out a faucet yourself!

How long will it take me? An hour or less

How much will it cost? It all depends on the kind of faucet you use. A washerless faucet made from brass or stainless steel (and coated with one of a variety of finishes, from nickel to chrome to bronze) ranges in price from $100 to $600 for really fancy versions. Choose one that suits the style of your bathroom.

What do I need? In addition to a new faucet that fits the opening you have (a single-piece or split unit), you'll need a few basic tools and materials:

8-inch adjustable wrench or 6-inch slip-joint pliers

Towel(s)

Penetrating oil lubricant

Solution of half vinegar and half water

Scouring pad

Clean rags

Plumber's putty or silicon caulk

How do I do it?

1. Turn off the two shutoff valves under the faucet you're replacing. Then, open the faucet and allow it to drain and release any pressure.

2. Disconnect the water supply lines from the faucet only.

3. Line the sink with one or more towels to protect it.

4. Remove the top-mount faucet from the sink. It's held in place by nuts that screw on to the tailpieces, so you're going to have to go "down under" the sink to loosen the nuts with pliers or a wrench. If it's a very old fixture and the nuts are rusted or corroded, apply penetrating oil lubricant and allow it to sit. Work according to the manufacturer's instructions before trying to remove the nuts.

5. Once the faucet has been removed, you'll most likely see a lot of gunk in the area where the faucet was attached. Clean it off before installing the new faucet. A solution of equal parts vinegar and water will help dissolve the buildup. Work it in with a scouring pad, then rinse and dry the area with a clean rag.

6. If your new faucet comes with a rubber or plastic gasket for the base, skip this step. If it does not, run a bead of plumber's putty or silicon caulk around the faucet's base.

7. Position the faucet, pressing it against the putty or gasket to ensure a good seal.

8. Install the washers and mounting nuts on the tailpieces under the sink. Tighten the nuts by hand.

9. Align the faucet with the back of the sink and tighten the mounting nuts with pliers or a wrench. If necessary, use another clean rag to wipe away excess caulk around the base.

10. Hook up the supply lines and turn on the water at the shutoff valves.

SHOWER POWER (AND TUBS, TOO)

Bathrooms have become retreat areas in our homes, and luxurious showers and bath-tubs play a big part in creating that spalike atmosphere. The most popular trend in bathrooms now is a separate shower and bathtub instead of the conventional tub/shower combo unit. If you have the space to create different bathing and showering zones, do it. It's a great investment that you will get a lot of use and pleasure out of.

Having a separate bathtub allows you more flexibility in choosing a bathtub style, too. You can choose a freestanding claw-foot tub or a relaxing built-in whirlpool. In fact, bathroom pros say the majority of us bathroom remodelers and builders say we want a whirlpool. So a spa tub is a nice extra that's worth the money if you can afford it. More and more manufacturers are entering the marketplace, so there is a wide variety of whirlpool tubs to choose from at a variety of price levels, although you can expect to pay at least three times more for a basic whirlpool tub with eight jets than you would for a standard tub, which can be bought for as little as $100 at home centers.

If you can't afford to replace your tub and shower, there are several things you can do to update and upgrade what you've got:

Replace small showerheads with large ones. Rainfall-style showerheads and large massaging heads are sought after—and with good reason. They impart invigo-rating, spalike luxury to the humble at-home shower.

Add an extra showerhead or two to your existing shower. Adding an extra head gives you a luxurious Swiss shower effect. You might have to change the size of the pipe to accommodate enough pressure, which could be expensive. You are also using a lot of water when you use multiple pow-erful showerheads, so you may want to add a filtration system to reuse water that would otherwise literally go down the drain. The

barbara's best bet

FIND YOUR OWN FIXTURES

Let the plumber supply the pipes, but save money by supplying the plumbing fixtures yourself. Plumbers mark up expensive tubs and other fixtures, just as electricians mark up light fixtures. And you can find what you really love instead of being limited by the plumber's selection.

head can be placed about 12 to 15 inches under the existing head or on the opposite wall, if the plumbing lines are available. A plumber needs to install this, and it may take several hours and cost several hundred dollars, but you'll end up with a unique shower for much less than it would have cost you to replace the unit wholesale. Note that you will probably have to replace the original showerhead so all of the heads match.

comfort zone

ADD AN EXTRA SHOWER

I love to take a brisk, hot shower in the morning or after a day at the beach. A self-contained shower is pretty economical, and small enough that you can fit one into spaces you might think are too small for this little luxury, such as an underused powder room or basement playroom. You need only about 1 square yard to install a shower, provided that there are an adequate water supply and drainage at hand. Turning a powder room or hallway washroom into a full bath—that's money in your pocket and a relief for your busy household! A basic fiberglass one-piece shower can be bought for about $300 to $500 at home improvement centers. Installation should take less than 1 day and, depending on how complicated the plumbing is (running water lines and so on), can cost from $300 to $500 or more.

Reglaze your tub. Reglazing a chipped or damaged tub is amazing. It can make a dingy, damaged hunk of porcelain or enameled cast iron look brand-new again. If you have a vintage tub, it's really worth having this done, because old tubs are so unique and often luxuriously deep. Reglazing costs between $300 and $500, depending on how large the tub is and where you live. But having it removed and replaced could cost much more.

Add a new lining. You can also cover your tub and reline your shower walls with new high-gloss acrylic bathtub or shower liners. They fit right over your old, worn, or damaged unit and do not disturb your existing tiles, flooring, and plumbing. Your bathtub or shower will be ready to use the same day at a cost of about $650 to $1,200 for the liner and installation, depending on the size of the job. That's just a portion of what it would cost to rip out and replace an exisiting tub and shower with new fixtures, which can cost $2,000 to $5,000. Use "tub and shower liners" as keywords to search online for manufacturers and installers.

—— on your own ——

Paint Tile for a Quick Fix

If you hate those 4 × 4-inch squares of pale pink tile but can't afford or don't have time for a total redo, there's hope—and it comes in a can. Painting tile is fairly simple, and the results will surprise you!

How long will it take me? Reserve a few hours over 2 days for this project. The primer and first coat need several hours to dry, so most likely you will be applying the second coat on day 2.

How much will it cost? Supplies and materials should cost under $25.

What do I need?

Blue painter's tape

Rubber gloves

A quart of primer specifically made for ceramic tile

A high-density foam brush for cutting in around edges and a high-density foam roller for smooth application over large areas. Make sure the brush and roller are appropriate for oil-based paint.

Turpentine for cleanup

A quart of paint specifically made for ceramic tile

How do I do it?

1. Clean the tile thoroughly and get rid of all grime, soap scum, mold, and mildew. Make sure the grout and the tiles are completely dry before you begin. If any of the grout needs to be repaired or replaced, remove it carefully with the end of a flat-head screwdriver and regrout it (see page 136 for information on grouting). Wait a day for the grout to dry thoroughly. Since you will be working with oil-based enamels, make sure the room is well ventilated. Open a window and turn on the bathroom fan. Use the painter's tape to protect any sections of the wall you don't plan on painting.

2. Wearing rubber gloves, paint the tile and grout with a primer made specifically for porcelain and ceramic tile. (You can also paint over plastic tiles, a type of wall covering especially popular in the 1950s.)

3. Clean your brushes with turpentine, following the manufacturer's instructions, and store them bristle-side up in a metal can to dry.

4. Let the primer dry completely, usually overnight.

5. Paint the tile and grout with the tile paint. Let the surface dry between coats. Two coats are usually needed.

ROYAL FLUSH

The old toilets in your house may look all right, but do they work well? Is the water always running? Do you have to jiggle the handle? Maybe you just need to replace a part and not the entire fixture. If one of the toilets in your home is not running properly and it's an old-fashioned flusher or an early version of a low-flow toilet, it might be costing you money. Replacing it is not that expensive and could save you a bundle on water bills.

Water usage laws changed in 1992, and toilet manufacturers started making low-flow versions that did not work so well. You had to flush them several times, which defeated the water-saving purpose. But now things have changed and the new low-flow toilets, mandated to save a precious and limited resource, are efficient and powerful. Older homes may have toilets that use up to 7 GPF (gallons per flush). Later water savers used 3.5 gallons, but new models now use only 1.6 gallons. Switching to one of these could save you from $50 to $100 a year on water and wastewater bills. Over time, that adds up.

No matter what style you prefer—modern, vintage, or traditional—you can find a standard-size toilet that fits with your home. Most are designed to fasten to the floor

12 inches from the wall, although models that attach 10 or 14 inches away are available. Check your existing sewer connection and attachment bolt placement before buying to make sure the model you choose will fit in the designated area of your bathroom. Toilet bowl height is standardized except for higher models designed for people with disabilities. Two bowl shapes are available: round and elongated. Traditional toilets are made from two pieces—a bowl and a water tank—but there are other options that center on the water tank:

- A one-piece toilet melds the water tank and bowl. They are easier to clean because there are fewer cracks to clean around, and they have a lower height, which allows them to be tucked under counters more easily.

- A wall-mounted toilet allows you to conceal the tank in the wall.

- A tankless toilet is one of the most popular must-haves for luxury bathrooms because of its sleek design and high-tech function. They rely on a powerful pump to provide exceptional flushing performance. These toilets are much more expensive than ordinary models (three or four times as much, in fact—well over $1,000). Tankless toilets can be installed at a standard 12-inch position. They usually do not require any special plumbing or electrical system hookups, because they use a standard $1/2$-inch water supply and a 120-volt GFCI outlet. You can also find models with self-closing lids and warm-water options for bidet-style washing.

ANATOMY OF A TOILET

Understanding what happens when you flush may help to demystify simple toilet repair. First, as you push down the handle, the chain inside the tank lifts the flapper valve. The water held in the tank flows through the flush valve opening into the toilet's bowl. The water from the tank forces the wastewater in the bowl through the trap (the U-shaped area under the bowl) and into the main drain. Once the tank is empty, the flapper valve seals the tank and the ball cock refills it. When the tank is full, the float ball shuts off the ball cock.

Ball cock. The water supply valve

Float ball. The ball that rides on the surface of the water in the tank. When the tank is full, the float ball shuts off the ball cock.

Flush valve. The connection that consists of the flapper and the flush valve seat

Flush valve seat. The brass or plastic sealant ring located at the bottom of the tank

Lift arm. The thin metal rod inside the tank that connects the flush handle to the flapper valve

Main drain. The slanting pipe in the basement or crawl space that carries wastewater to a sewer or septic tank

Main water valve. The knob, located on the wall near the floor, that you twist to turn on and off the water supply

Overflow pipe. The long, hollow tube fastened to the bottom of the tank

Flapper valve. The rubbery plug attached to the lift chain

Tank. The large ceramic container behind the toilet bowl that fills with and holds the water used for each flush

Trap. The U-shaped canal wastewater goes into as it leaves the toilet bowl

GET ORGANIZED

The only thing I love more than a beautiful bathroom is an orderly one! For me, there's no worse start to my day than having to get ready at a cluttered vanity. And you can be sure that the same cluttered vanity will make home buyers think twice. If your bathroom works well and looks good but lacks pizzazz, personality, and organization, a simple system that's pretty and practical will make life so much easier and more enjoyable. Here are some ways to straighten up with style and turn your bathroom into a destination worth spending time in:

- Pile pretty boxes on a shelf or in the linen closet to keep small, unattractive, or personal items out of sight. Look for ones made of water-resistant materials like plastic, glass, metal, stainless steel, or laminated paper. Plain paper or cardboard boxes can warp and bubble in moist areas. Wood boxes may expand and contract, making lids stick. Wicker baskets collect dust and aren't that easy to clean. Wire or metal baskets are much easier to clean, and those made of wire collect less dust in the generally larger crevices of their weave.

- Stack towel bars and racks on a wall or door for maximum and neat easy-access storage with an upscale-hotel flair. An even better choice is a towel rack that combines a shelf with two or three bars. Keep extra towels, shampoos, and soaps in a spalike arrangement on the shelf. The bars are handy for drying damp towels.

- Add a small chair for a dressing-room effect. It will double as a step stool and a surface for laying your towels or clothes on when you're using the bathroom, and you can sit on it, of course, while dressing yourself or drying off a child. Wooden chairs should be very well constructed and painted with a gloss paint suitable for bathrooms. Metal chairs should be free of rust and powder coated with waterproof paint. If your chair has an upholstered seat, cover it with easy-to-clean real or faux leather, canvas, or terry (use a large towel for the fabric if you can't find terry yard goods).

- An extra wall cabinet placed over the toilet or anywhere in the bathroom can store toiletries such as shampoos, bar soap, washcloths, and cotton balls.

- Open shelves over the toilet or above a towel bar provide space for bath salts, pretty soaps, personal mementos, or plants. Remember, plants bring life, cheer, and oxygen to a room!

- A shallow bookcase (less than 12 inches) is a wonderful piece of furniture for a bathroom if you have enough space. The shelves can hold boxes of bath essentials, neatly stacked books and magazines, and rolled hand towels. The top of the bookcase can serve as another surface for a plant and a clock (you'll never be late again!). Give bookcases two or three coats of a gloss paint for durability and easy cleanup.

- A magazine rack is a good alternative if a bookcase is too much for a small bathroom. Metal and wood racks are easy to find at flea markets and antique shops. A fresh coat of bathroom paint makes them functional and easy to clean.

- Hooks affixed to a wall or door can keep bathrobes, clothes, and towels off the floor. For super strength, install the hooks into wall studs using a hammer. If that isn't possible, use wall anchors in drywall or over-the-door hooks for hollow-core doors.

- Decorative trays are a wonderful way to keep like items together in an orderly and attractive fashion. Depending on the style of your bathroom, glass, painted tin, stainless steel, plastic, wood, chrome, silver, aluminum, and brass are all good material choices. Group together brushes, combs, and hair clips and bands on one tray. Makeup essentials, cotton swabs, and cotton balls can go on another. Just be sure to place items in containers that are similar in style and color to the tray. That will create a neat, stylish look. In addition, you will be able to easily see what needs replenishing, cleaning, or replacing.

———————— ! ————————

Can you imagine having a bathroom that leads to the great outdoors? Nowadays, people want seamless transitions between the inside and outside. And why not, since the landscaping of your property is so valuable. Usable outdoor spaces like patios, lawns, decks, and other landscaped features extend your living space and give you a place to entertain, play, and simply relax and enjoy nature and the fresh air. Now let's take it outside!

!

CHAPTER 8

Curb Appeal

When I bought my first home, I'll admit that I didn't recognize the value or the significance of the trees, shrubs, and flowers that surrounded it. In fact, there were some odd-looking trees on the property that I very much took for granted. I thought they were just run-of-the-mill trees, nothing special. Boy, was I mistaken! Luckily I found a good landscaper who informed me that they were *specimen trees*, meaning that a landscaper had planted them in very particular places so people could get the greatest possible enjoyment from looking at their color, texture, and shape. They would have cost thousands of dollars to replace. As my knowledge grew and matured, I began to understand not only the real estate value of great landscaping, but also the lifestyle value—the beauty and tranquility that I now feel every time I step outside my door. My appreciation for landscaping has grown—just like the trees!

Landscaping is the picture frame around your home. Just as the wrong frame can diminish a stunning piece of artwork, the right frame elevates the painting's beauty. In much the same way, landscaping can truly showcase your home. A beautiful main entrance and front lawn are assets that pull visitors in and say, "Come and stay a while," while a lovely backyard beckons to those inside to come out and play. Don't send the wrong message by neglecting to maintain the exterior of your property or by letting its green areas "go to pot." Permanent features that extend living space also add tremendous value. Decks, porches, patios, walkways, paths, gazebos, gates, fences, play stations for the kids, and outbuildings should be useful, attractive, and fit in with the overall look of the house.

It does not all have to come together at once. Look at your outdoor space as a work in progress, an evolving expression of your feelings about the environment through different colors and shapes of flowers, grasses, shrubs, and trees, mixed with various stones, decks, and patios. I always think of four of the five senses when I consider making improvements to any outdoor space: sight, smell, touch, and sound. First I think of what visually pleases me as I approach my home, including the color it's painted and the kinds of flowers, shrubs, and trees that surround it. Plantings should also offer a pleasing fragrance, from the aromas of an herb garden strategically placed near the kitchen door to the exotic perfume of gardenias and heady scents of lilacs and roses. Textures should be varied—the combination of a smooth gravel driveway next to a grass or white clover lawn looks pretty, and both are pleasing underfoot. Finally, I think about what sounds I can add—from simple wind chimes and rain chains to fountains and falls that bring the soothing sound of running water to the landscape. The landscape around my house means everything to Zachary and me—and it is the most important feature of my property. As soon as I put down my things after arriving home, we run outside to jump in the pool or play in the leaves or snow.

A manicured landscape and a well-maintained home exterior are great for your bank account, too. Most people buying homes today want beautiful and easy-to-care-for grounds they can use just as they would another room in their house. That's why home landscaping is the third most important feature (after kitchens and baths) that buyers consider when property shopping. Did you know that a well-kept home with beautiful landscaping can realize a sales price that's at least 10 percent higher or even much more than comparable homes with average landscaping? That means you can add $20,000 or more to the value of a $200,000 house simply by beautifying its exterior features.

You can accomplish so many valuable enhancements yourself. For instance, just by placing small evergreens and undemanding flowers in pretty pots and planters, the look of your deck or porch can change dramatically. Go to the pros for more involved changes, such as establishing sweeping planting beds or building decks and patios to add even more architectural oomph to a site.

Don't limit your imagination! No matter what the size of your home or your budget, there are all sorts of things you can do to add curb appeal and cultivate your investment. Let's get started!

go to the pros

HIRING A LANDSCAPE ARCHITECT

You may want to make dramatic changes to your landscape—add large planting beds, put in a swimming pool and spa, or build outbuildings and patios. The best way to execute a major outdoor project is with the help of a landscape architect. You may think a landscape architect is only for people with large estates or a lot of money—not true! There are many landscape architects who specialize in small backyards and terrace gardens or larger suburban yards.

Who are these people?

A landscape architect is a person who plans, designs, and oversees the construction of gardens and outdoor structures. They know how to bring disparate outdoor elements, like greenery, hardscape, and buildings and other structures, into a unified whole. They understand the unique demands and characteristics of outdoor spaces. Their expertise about what plants and trees will work in your area is also invaluable. Moreover, they supervise the project to ensure that the landscaping and hardscaping crews execute the plans properly.

Where do I find them?

The best way to find a landscape architect is by asking friends or neighbors whose landscaping you like who did the work for them. Interview at least three prospects, look at their past work, talk to their clients, and then make a judgment based on that information. Better yet, drive around your neighborhood and, when you find landscapes you love, ask if a professional designed it. If you have trouble getting personal recommendations, consult the American Society of Landscape Architects (ASLA) for a list of registered landscape architects in your area. If you want to change the landscaping of a historic home, check with your local historical society or historic zoning board for the names of approved professionals who are familiar with local historical preservation rules.

What kind of training and certification do they need?

Landscape architects must have a 4-year professional landscape architecture degree and at least 4 years of experience to be licensed in many states (although rules vary by region). Licensed landscape architects have also passed the national landscape architecture licensing examination. Look for "RLA" (Registered Landscape Architect) on business cards. Verify the licensing and other credentials by calling ASLA and the licensing board in your community (or in the community in which the architect has an office).

How do I hire one?

It's similar to the process used in hiring an architect, which was discussed in Chapter 5. You'll want to call at least three and ask if they would be interested in working with you on a project. Give them some details on the scope of the project so they have an idea of the size. Always ask if they charge a fee for an initial interview; some do and some don't, but whether or not they charge is not an indication of the quality of their work. If you are meeting with a large firm, be sure to ask if more than one person will be assigned to your project and ask to meet the entire team. You will be spending a lot of time with your architect, so you should be sure you enjoy working with him or her. Listen to your instincts—do you feel a connection? Does he or she understand and relate to what you want?

Next, determine what the landscape architects' design philosophy and favorite styles are. Ask each one how long he or she thinks the project will take to complete and discuss fees and anticipated construction costs. A landscape architect's fee can range from 10 to 15 percent of the total cost of the project, which includes design fees, labor, materials (plants, topsoil, stone, and other hardscape features), plumbing, lighting, and trash and debris removal. Ask for references from past clients and call them! Visit at least one project by each landscape architect.

Finally, make sure that any landscape architect you are considering can work within your time frame. Ask if he or she can complete the project by a certain date—if you have one in mind. Landscape crews are very busy from spring through fall. The best time to meet with a landscape architect and book a job is during seasonal downtimes, like winter. In warmer climates, because landscaping can be done throughout the year, crews may not be as booked up during traditional planting seasons, but in areas of the country where growing seasons are short, booking in advance is a necessity.

What about the contract?

The landscape architect draws up a contract. The contract for design services is a legal document that binds you and the landscape architect for the term of the project. Take your time in reviewing the contract to make sure that everything you discussed is listed. Remember, you don't have to sign anything you don't agree with. Contracts vary by state, but here is what you should expect to see:

- The name and address of the landscape project

- A brief description of services to be provided by the landscape architect. It could be as simple as "Build a pond and waterfall with an adjacent patio and small birch forest in the backyard; lay turf and foundation plantings with perennial garden in the front yard."

- The name, address, and license number of the landscape architect and the name and address of the client

- The amount of the retainer fee (money you give the landscape architect to get started on the project) and a detailed accounting of how it will be spent

- The total price for completing the project, the method of payment, and the schedule of payments as agreed upon by both parties, including the amount of the payment due upon completion of the project. Final payment should not be made until the project is done and you are satisfied.

- A notice that reads: "Landscape architects are licensed by the State of _____" (your state goes in the blank)

- A description of the process that the landscape architect and you will use if you request additions or major changes to the agreed-upon plan during the course of the project

- A list of the costs that are not included in the stated fee. For example, you may have to take care of having a portion of your house cleaned or repainted after the workers leave if it was soiled during the project. If it's a backyard project, the architect may want to specifically state that no work will be done to the side or front of the house.

- A statement that says your approval is required before additional costs can be incurred. This is very important; you'll want to see every bill associated with material and labor costs for your project.

- A statement that says that your written approval is required before the landscape architect can proceed with each phase of the work

- An outline detailing the procedure either of you can use to terminate the agreement before design services are completed and another describing the procedure for handling disputes between parties should the need arise

- Your responsibilities during the life of the contract, such as granting access to your property so the crews can do their work

- A statement about whether you or the landscape architect owns the landscape architectural documents and plans

- A list of subcontractors to be used and copies of their workers' compensation agreements and insurance policies

- Both of you should sign and date two copies of the agreement. You should keep one original copy and the landscape architect will keep the other.

Recordkeeping does not end with the signed contract. You have to keep a written record of all verbal communications relating to the project that you have with the architect and crew. After you talk to the landscape architect about the project, follow up with a written memo recounting the important aspects of the conversation, and keep a copy of the note for your records. If you are very organized, you may want to write memos or notes to yourself about the progress of your project. And take pictures. Visually documenting the stages of the project is useful if a problem or disagreement arises, plus having pictures of the area taken before, during, and after the work is done is a wonderful way to record the transformation of your yard.

The architect will then come up with a set of final plans and architectural drawings—and sometimes even engineered drawings, depending on your local building codes and requirements—to secure work permits. The plans will include notations for the existing and any planned water, sewer, gas, and electrical lines. Property lines are also clearly delineated. He or she will also put an RLA (Registered Landscape Architect) stamp on the final drawings to indicate that he or she is registered or licensed to practice. That's essential when applying for permits—most communities require them if major excavation and building are parts of your project. The community office that issues permits wants to see that the drawings were done by a professional landscape architect. They are especially concerned about water, gas, and electrical lines being protected if major digging is required.

The landscape architect's job ends when the project is complete. He or she can give you a 1-year guarantee for the life of plants, but it probably will be contingent upon their having received proper care. If you or someone you hire does not take care of plantings properly, the plants will die. The architect and landscaping crew cannot take responsibility for your neglect. If a newly planted mature tree dies because it was diseased, you can usually get your money back or have the tree replaced within the first growing year. But remember that gardens require the loving hands of their keepers, and that care is up to you. The architect may be able to recommend gardeners if you do not want to do the maintenance yourself, or you may even be able to hire his or her own company for maintenance and therefore get a longer guarantee on the life of the plants.

HARDWORKING HARDSCAPE

As I said earlier, there are many things you can do to improve the outside of your house. Basic maintenance, like keeping the lawn green and mowed and the shrubs neatly pruned, is a no-brainer. Structural changes and additions can also make a big difference in how you use and enjoy your little plot of green. Here are some of my favorite features:

STREET STYLE: THE DRIVEWAY

Driveways are a neglected area of the home. I think it's because most of the time we spend on them is when we're driving over them in our cars. We rarely take the time to notice what they look like, and as a result they can become unkempt. Yet your driveway is an integral part of your landscape.

Check the surface condition. Concrete is expensive, as is black asphalt, and both are functional, so it may be worth fixing any problems rather than removing the driveway if it is made of these materials. However, if your concrete or asphalt driveway is in very bad disrepair, it might be worthwhile to have it broken up and removed. A pea gravel driveway is very pretty, and more appealing than concrete or asphalt. It makes a satisfying crunching sound under tires and feet, too. Cobblestones and paving stones are beautiful and turn a driveway into a grand entrance, but material and labor costs make them expensive. "Green" driveways that combine a tough turf with concrete or pavers are elegant.

OPEN AND SHUT CASE: GARAGE DOORS

I prefer that a garage be tucked away to the side or back of a house so the front door takes center stage. However, many new houses, such as mine, have the garage door right up front or on the L of the house—even some older homes have the garage door next to the front door. If that's your situation, you know that the garage door's huge expanse of white can really dominate a house. One way to give the exterior of your house a lift is by replacing a plain garage door with a stylish version that suits the look of your home. It would be costly and perhaps even structurally impossible to move the garage, so if you can't eliminate it, decorate it! Make a front-facing garage a focal point. Garage door styles range from modern and sleek to old-fashioned and charming. They can mimic the look of barn doors or an archway on a French country carriage house, or evoke the Space Age with panels that combine solid material in primary colors and glass windows.

Like kitchen cabinets, garage doors come in stock, semi-custom, and custom versions. Stock doors, ready to hang, come in a fairly limited range of materials, panel designs, and number of windows. A basic, unpainted two-car-garage door made from pressed wood or steel with recessed panels and eight glass windows plus new tracks and rollers will cost around $1,000. Installation is extra. Any upgrades you make, such as increasing the number of windows or substituting decorative panels, add to the cost.

A semi-custom door gives you more style options. Manufacturers offer a variety of mix-and-match features that enable you to create something that looks unique. There are a wider variety of woods to choose from at this level, including cedar and mahogany. There is also a wide selection of glass styles that range from antique-looking bubble glass to frosted panels and even stained glass. A semi-custom wood door with new tracks and rollers can cost from $1,500 to $4,000, depending on materials. Semi-custom steel doors cost a bit less.

Custom doors cost substantially more than the stock varieties but may be worth it if you want to change the look of your house without making major structural changes. The sky is the limit with a custom door, but expect to pay upward of $5,000 or more. Whatever kind of door you buy, make sure it comes with guarantees on workmanship, parts, and materials.

FRONT DOOR STORY

Another remarkable way to dress up your house without tearing it down and starting over is by painting or replacing the front door. A great front door is like a gorgeous string of beads worn with a simple dress: It brightens up the entire design and makes it look new—and "new" houses are worth more than old ones. My door is 9 feet tall and made of cherry. I love the way it looks—very dramatic. If your door is sturdy and in good condition but looks a bit tired, wake it up with a color chosen to complement but contrast with your house or trim color. Sand the door first, then clean it to remove any dust and grime. Prime it with an exterior-grade primer and then paint it with a gloss or high-gloss exterior paint for durability and easy cleaning.

If your door is in good shape and doesn't need repainting or staining, consider changing its standard-issue hardware to something more substantial and stylish. Details such as beautiful brass, wrought iron or brushed nickel knobs, a wide kick-plate, and a whimsical or designer doorknocker and bell buzzer will add sparkle to your entrance and impress potential buyers, too.

A brand-new door custom-designed to make a style statement is also an option. If your existing door is drab or damaged, investing in a high-quality door is worthwhile. However, be careful not to overdress your house with a door that's far more modern, elaborate, or ornate than the house itself. Don't veer too far from your home's style. For example, resist the temptation to put a Victorian-looking door with an oval of leaded glass on a modern ranch house. By the same token, a modern mahogany masterpiece will look out of place on a Garrison colonial. Consider adding sidelights, narrow windows that flank one or both sides of the door. They create a grander, more welcoming entrance. Be sure your entryway is clean and inviting; including a container garden and a chair is a simple way to enhance a small entryway, and even a single shrub in a pretty pot adds life to modest-looking front steps.

ALL DECKED OUT: DECKS, PORCHES, AND PATIOS

Decks create a usable transition between the interior and exterior of a house, making them one of the landscaping features buyers most want because they extend the interior space and serve as extra square footage during the mild-weather months. You can add a basic 16 × 20-foot deck with built-in benches and even a couple of planter boxes to your home for about $7,000 in most parts of the country, although prices vary by region. Treated wood is a popular construction material, as well as the most affordable. You can also use some of the newer products on the market that are a composite of wood and plastic. This decking material is extremely durable, does not require annual staining or sealing, and is fade resistant and easy to walk on (no splinters!). Composite materials, some of which very convincingly imitate wood grains, are more expensive than wood but can last much longer.

A deck that extends off the kitchen, family room, or the front of the house expands your entertaining space. Add a roof and some posts to a front deck and it takes on the traditional look of an old-fashioned porch. Line the ceiling with bead-board paneling and paint it blue. Ceiling fans transform it into a room that will be enjoyed on hot summer afternoons and sultry evenings.

Like a deck, a flagstone, brick, or concrete patio that communicates with the living room or kitchen adds living space to a home. Laying pavers in sand is less costly than permanently affixing stones in cement, but a patio laid in a cement foundation can someday be enclosed to become a sunroom or screened-in porch.

WALK THIS WAY

Paths that lead the way from the house and deck to patios and gardens are another feature that adds value to the landscape. I built a flagstone path to the backyard along the side of my house. I also have more casual pea gravel, stepping-stone, and Mexican river rock walkways, as well. Varying the texture of paths by using different materials or combining materials (bricks and cobblestones, pea gravel surrounding dyed concrete stepping-stones) adds further interest. Depending on the topography of your yard, laying a path could be a do-it-yourself job. If the land is very hilly and rocky, you may have to hire professional help to dig and move the earth and lay the heavy materials. A path covered with mulch or gravel can be installed on your own. To be comfortable for walking, most paths need to be at least 3 feet wide. Place walkways away from the main growth area of large or important trees because their roots will disturb the walkway, plus you could smother the root system with the path material. Determine the growth area by looking at the diameter of the uppermost part of the tree and place your path at least 6 feet *beyond* that. Dig down at least 2 or 3 inches, smooth and level the ground with a rake, and get rid of any stray roots you discover (removing these root tendrils will not damage the tree if you are far enough away from it). Remove large stones and rocks. If you are laying gravel, make a bed with landscaping cloth topped off with an inch of construction sand. For a more casual mulch path—great for edging garden beds—place mulch in a thick layer over landscaping cloth. Landscaping cloth—usually a black mesh with tiny holes that allow for drainage but discourage weed growth—can be found at your local garden center or in most gardening supply catalogs.

A SHOW OF LIGHT

Exterior lighting is an essential part of any landscaping project—how else are you going to enjoy nighttime entertaining or find your way to the front door on a dark, rainy night? At its best, lighting is both decorative and practical. Lights can be installed on decks and patios, along pathways, next to or above doorways, and on outbuildings. Spotlights can be used to highlight a beautiful specimen tree, like a Japanese maple, or a garden's architectural features, such as a statue, stone wall, or gate. A series of small lights will help visitors find their way to your front door or up steps. Step lights installed flush with the surface gently wash the surface of each step in light, without glare. Dramatic lighting is also a pleasure to view from inside your house, particularly if it helps to showcase a gazebo, fountain, pretty garden shed, or any other special feature on your property.

Security lights strategically placed at each corner of your house bathe your yard in bright light. At the minimum, your house should be equipped with a set of these simple floodlights. You can buy units that are controlled by motion detectors or manually. If you live in a suburban or rural area, like I do, deer and other creatures can trip the motion sensors and splash your lawn with light all night long if you are not careful to install them so they detect only motion closer to the house (where animals will sometimes tread, but rarely so).

There are two kinds of outdoor lights: low voltage and line voltage. You see a lot of solar-powered lights in the marketplace, but they are very weak in terms of lighting strength and are not recommended if you want to really light an area. Even for ambient lighting, you are better off using low-voltage models. Some decorative solar lights can be expensive and don't offer much bang for your buck.

Low-Voltage Lighting

Low-voltage lights have the advantage of being inexpensive and less disruptive to the surrounding landscape because their electrical cables can be simply covered with mulch or buried in a shallow trench rather than in a deeper trench, as line-voltage lights must be. You can buy a set of 8 or 10 lights for about $60 at a home improvement center or large discount retailer. The fixtures are usually small, unobtrusive, and plastic (and therefore light—no pun intended!), so do-it-yourself installation is possible. Usually these lights do not require another circuit to be installed to operate. They can be hard-wired into the existing household circuit or simply plugged into an outdoor outlet. A transformer that comes with the lights reduces the household 120 volts to 12.

And that's the big drawback with low-voltage lights—their low power. They don't provide a very bright glow and can be downright dim. In fact, they get less powerful if they are installed more than 75 feet from the transformer, which in most yards is not very far. Plus, inexpensive plastic products don't last long and may need to be replaced after just one foul-weather season.

Line-Voltage Lighting

Line voltage provides strong light over long distances. You also have a lot more choice with line-voltage lights since they come in many styles and sizes, from up lights, which direct a beam of light upward, to pathway lights, to lampposts. However, line-voltage lighting requires professional installation by a licensed electrician. Since the cables must be buried in narrow trenches, labor costs also apply. That means that on the low end, it can cost around $500 to put in a basic line-voltage lighting system—and it goes up from there depending on how complex you want your system to be. It is a big job, but a fairly permanent one. Once it's done, it's done for a long while. Major changes to the system mean paying the electrician for a return trip, so plan wisely. If you want to install a line-voltage lighting system, it's a good idea to talk to a landscape lighting consultant, who can help you devise a plan that can be added to over time without making changes to the current installations. Your landscape architect may also include a lighting program with his or her design.

—— on your own ——

Replace Exterior Lights

Lanterns that flank entryways both light the area and act as decorative accents that reinforce the style and look of your home. Changing old, unattractive, or outdated fixtures with new, prettier versions is a great way to affordably brighten up your house. Replacement is crucial if the existing fixtures have corroded. Luckily, it's really easy to do.

How long will it take me? Just about an hour

How much will it cost? It depends on what kind of light fixtures you buy. You can find a nice pair of good-quality exterior lights for less than $200.

What do I need?

Safety glasses

Flathead and Phillips head screwdrivers

Electric circuit tester

Wire strippers

Crimping tool

Mounting bracket with threaded center bolt (this should come with the new fixture, or you can use the bracket from the old fixture if it is in good condition)

Tape measure

Light fixtures approved for outdoor use (you can use outdoor fixtures indoors, but it is not safe to use indoor fixtures on the exterior of your house)

Drill with screwdriver bits

Waterproof exterior-grade caulk

How do I do it?

Follow the manufacturer's instructions that come with your light fixture, but here's what you can expect:

1. Turn off the power at the service panel.

2. Unscrew the light fixture from the house. You may have to pry off the screw cap covers to expose the screws. You can do this with a flathead screwdriver. Behind the light fixture you will see a junction box. Test the wiring with the electric circuit tester to make sure the power is off.

3. Loosen the collar that holds the three wires in place. Disconnect the wiring that leads to the existing fixture. For safety, disconnect the powered black wire first, the neutral white wire next, and the bare ground wire last.

4. Use the wire stripper to remove about ⅝ inch of insulation from the end of each wire.

5. Attach the ground wire of your new fixture to the one in the junction box using a barrel crimp connector or wire nut included in the light kit, which is required by building codes. Then attach the remaining wires, white to white and black to black, with the wire nuts included in the light kit.

6. Install the bracket from your light kit (or reuse the original one) by attaching it to the junction box using a screwdriver, and then insert the wires through the collar.

7. Fasten the light fixture base to the junction box, install the lightbulb, and turn on the power at the service panel. Test the light. If the light works properly, remove the lightbulb and attach the light fixture cover to the base with the appropriate screwdriver.

8. Caulk around the edges of the light fixture to keep water out.

SHED SPREAD: OUTBUILDINGS

Outbuildings equal storage space and storage space equals value. People are always looking for more room to store their stuff, and sheds are a great option. Many people use their garage for storing everything from holiday ornaments to out-of-season clothes to sporting equipment. A shed frees up your garage for cars and perhaps even an at-home workshop.

Home improvement super centers sell large plastic sheds. While they are practical and moveable, I don't think they are as appealing as wooden sheds that can be painted to match or coordinate with your home. I have a friend who installed a 100-square-foot wooden shed with double barn doors and two windows with shutters for $1,500. She added window boxes under each small window to complete the look. That simple shed added to the selling price of her home. She's not going anywhere quite yet, so she uses it to store garden tools, seasonal items, and bicycles.

Maintain outbuildings and sheds as well as you do your home. It's a big turnoff to see rundown sheds or barns on an otherwise well-kept piece of property. Keep them neat and organized on the inside as well, especially if you are considering selling. Plywood shelves hung on simple metal brackets keep smaller items in place, while metal hooks and plastic barrels corral larger items such as rakes and shovels.

comfort zone

CREATE A GREEN SCREEN

If you are looking for privacy from the neighbors or just want to create a cozy outdoor room, a natural privacy screen is so much prettier than a stockade fence. Many fast-growing cultivars—such as holly, privet, and blue spruce—are ideal for creating privacy. Different types of plants have different soil requirements, but generally they are all planted the same way. For each plant, dig a hole twice the diameter of its root ball and deep enough so the top of the ball ends up just above the surrounding grade. Put the ball in the hole, fill the space with soil you removed, place mulch around the trunk, and water it heavily. Remember not to plant too close to your property line, because you'll need permanent access to both sides for care and pruning. Plant at least 10 feet away to allow ample room for growth and access.

ALL FENCED IN

You've probably heard the expression "good fences make good neighbors," and there is a reason that is true. Most people cherish their privacy, and fences, whether made of wood, stone, or evergreen hedges, create a sense of boundary and shelter. It is not necessary or even practical to fence in the entire perimeter of your yard. But fencing off a portion of your backyard or perhaps a patio off the master bedroom is one way of defining private spaces and adding interest to the landscape. You can choose an interesting way to set the pickets (uneven or scalloped tops, for example) or add a decorative gate. Painted picket fences should be inspected yearly and painted if necessary. Any damaged parts should be repaired or replaced as soon as possible.

CHILDREN'S PLAY AREAS

Zachary loves his swing set. It provides countless hours of fun for him, for his friends, and for me. A swing set anchored securely into ground that has been padded with a thick layer of mulch or playground-quality rubber padding is a wonderful play area for your children. Even a simple swing tied with heavy-duty rope to the sturdy branches of a friendly tree brings hours of pleasure to kids and adults alike—and it's a charming addition to the landscape. (It's pretty easy to make a tree swing yourself, too.) Other kid-friendly features, like a small vegetable garden, basketball court, and badminton court, encourage kids to get outdoors, experience nature, and get some fresh air and exercise.

GRILL THRILLS

I love to entertain outdoors. I may not be a great cook on the inside, but when I head outside, watch out: I am the Grill Master! If you're like me, you should make a grill center part of your outdoor experience. You don't have to go over the top, however, unless you are really into outdoor cooking. It can be a pricey pastime: Commercial-quality stainless-steel grills start at about $1,000 and go up from there. Expect to spend at least another $2,500 on a custom-built tile, stone, or brick structure to house your grill and provide counter space. Accessories such as storage cabinets and a refrigerator give you a full-fledged outdoor kitchen for $7,000. An elaborate outdoor kitchen might be a real benefit in southern climates. I live in the Northeast, so a complete outdoor kitchen with a built-in barbecue and fireplace isn't something I would get a lot of use out of for more than a few months a year. If you want to extend outdoor entertainment into the chillier months, a propane patio heater is a must. These tall, powerful units make dining alfresco in November possible—even in New York.

SWIMMING POOLS, SPAS, AND HOT TUBS

I love my swimming pool and would not be without one. Zach and I spend countless hours in it on summer weekends, and he loves to invite his friends over for pool parties after a day at the beach. I have my own grown-up pool parties, too—and there's nothing like taking a dip on a hot night. I also live in an area that is considered by many to be a vacation community, and a pool is a really desirable property feature in such areas. In warmer regions of the country, such as California, Arizona, and Florida, pools and spas are nearly a necessity. Adding a pool in cooler regions is something you do if you really love to swim. Some people think it's a negative feature, especially if they have very young children. That makes a pool optional—but very nice, nonetheless. Built-in pools can be expensive—for excavation, preparation, and filling the pool with water, as well as basic landscaping, expect to pay at least $12,000 for a vinyl pool and $25,000 and up for a 20 × 40-foot gunite pool. A lot of communities require pools to be fenced in (and you should require it too, for safety), adding even more to the expense.

A less expensive and more broadly appealing alternative to a swimming pool is a hot tub or spa tub. Find them at specialty spa stores and home centers. A four-person spa starts at around $2,600 for an aboveground model and goes up to $15,000 for a gunite hot tub that's sunk into the ground like a swimming pool. The prices go up from there, based on the size and features included (some pricey luxury hot tubs include flat-screen TVs and beverage centers). Hot tubs can be placed on top of a deck or patio, sunk into the ground, or placed into a cutout made in a deck. The more complicated the installation, the higher the labor costs, which start at $500 and go up from there depending on how much digging, cutting, and electrical and plumbing work is required.

WATER WORKS

I happen to love outdoor showers and consider them very practical—I have one in my backyard and whenever I use it, it gives me the feeling of being in one of the many warm, exotic places I have traveled to. An outdoor shower can be a simple contraption hooked up to a garden hose or an elaborate enclosure plumbed for hot and cold running water. Either way, a shower is not nearly as expensive to install as a pool or a hot tub, and it's a wonderful feature to have if you have children. Believe me, it's great to have a dedicated area to "hose off" children who've been digging in the sand, making mud pies, or just running around outside in the summer. For adults, a cool shower under the stars on a steamy summer night—it's a simple yet sublime pleasure. There are those who may disagree with me, but I think an outdoor shower is an asset when selling a house—although buyers may not even know they want one until they see it. It's one of those little luxuries that make a house distinctive and memorable. The enclosure should be attractive and blend seamlessly into the landscape. I enclosed mine with inexpensive bamboo fencing, but you can also create a cedar or redwood enclosure or plant tall hedges for a natural "shower room." Add a bench and some Japanese stones on the floor to really make it comfortable and spalike.

go to the pros

PAINTING THE HOUSE

With the exception of most vinyl siding, exterior cladding must be painted every 5 to 7 years, and more often if your house endures harsh weather and is not protected from sun, wind, and rain by large trees. New tract or development homes may need to be painted after only a few years, since they are often covered with a single coat of paint. They often lack substantial landscaping as well, leaving them completely exposed to the elements, so you may have to repaint every few years until nearby trees and shrubs mature sufficiently to shade and shield the house from the elements.

My house is postmodern and clad in cedar shingles. They are silvery gray and crisp against white trim—a look very typical for the area. Other houses in my neighborhood are traditional painted clapboard. We all take a lot of pride in keeping our homes maintained and fresh looking. That means keeping the exterior paint in good condition. While I do not have to paint the shingles on my house (they require another kind of regular care), I do make sure the trim always looks its best.

Who does it?

Painting a house is a job for professional house painters. When selecting a painter, ask for three estimates from established local firms that are familiar with the weather conditions of and exterior materials commonly used in your area. Request references—fly-by-night painting companies are, unfortunately, all too common. It's better to hire a painting company that has been in business for several years in the same location. A very low bid is a warning sign that the person may not be a professional or will use shoddy materials (and as a result your house will need repainting in a year or so).

How long does it take?

Depending on the size of your house, it can take anywhere from 1 to 3 weeks. A 2,500-square-foot house, for example, should take about 3 to 7 days to complete.

How much will it cost?

Painting a house costs several thousand dollars for labor alone. In addition, established contractors and painting specialists have credit accounts with their paint and material suppliers, so the cost of materials will be included in the final bill. A nonprofessional may ask you to pay for his materials before he starts working, so be careful not to choose someone who will end up running out on you.

When seeking bids, ask each contractor for a rundown of how the crew will prepare the house and surrounding areas before painting, how many coats of paint they will give the house, what brand of paint will be used, and how long the work is guaranteed for. For example, contractors who offer painting as part of an array of general household repair and renovation services don't always protect the shrubs and lawn around your house with burlap drop cloths unless they are asked to. If you don't ask before they begin work, you and your expensive hedges may be in for a costly surprise. A good paint job should include the use of a well-applied high-quality paint as well as a complete power wash, thorough caulking of any cracks or openings, and any necessary scraping or sanding of old or peeling paint. Shutters, flower boxes, and other removable components, which should be taken off before the house is painted, must be prepped, painted, and then reinstalled when all surfaces have dried thoroughly.

What happens?

Once you have checked the company's references and accepted a bid, ask for copies of the painter's license (or a home improvement license), workman's compensation documentation, and general liability policy and make sure you are individually covered. If you hire an unlicensed, uninsured contractor and he gets injured on the job, you will be responsible for any medical and rehabilitation bills.

on your own

Perform an Exterior Inspection

It doesn't matter if your house is clad in wood, stucco, vinyl, masonry, or other siding: All exteriors must be cleaned and inspected for damage at least twice a year. I inspect mine in the spring and fall so any damage can be corrected before very hot or cold weather sets in. Allowing problems to develop unchecked is detrimental to your home's appearance and value.

How long will it take me? About an hour

How much will it cost? Nothing!

What do I need? Take a clipboard, paper, and a pen with you so you can record what you see—and make a note of any needed repairs. I also recommend wearing a pair of old jeans, a work shirt, and comfortable boots or shoes.

How do I do it? Start at the top and work your way down.

Roof. From the ground, check for missing or broken shingles and have them replaced immediately. I strongly advise against using a ladder to get on the roof—leave that exercise to a roofing expert. If your home is 25 or more years old, you may have to eventually replace the roof entirely, which can cost upward of $5,000 depending on the size of the roof and the type of shingles you use. It is also worthwhile to periodically hire a handyman or general landscape maintenance company to remove any branches and other debris from the roof. Moss indicates the presence of moisture, but it is not necessarily detrimental to your roof. If you see an abundance of moss or other greenery growing on your roof, consult a roofing expert.

Gutters and downspouts. Look for debris on top of the gutter. This may indicate that the gutter contains leaves, sticks, and other obstructions that can restrict water flow away from the foundation. If the gutters appear to be clogged, have them cleaned out by a specialist (look for "Gutters" in the phone book) and consider having them covered with a mesh gutter guard, which discourages leaves and twigs from settling in.

Cladding and foundation. If you have wood siding, check it for warped or rotted areas. Look for peeling paint or exposed wood. If you have a brick, stone, or stucco house, look for cracked or chipped masonry and mortar. You can make simple patches with patching compounds specifically made for masonry or stucco that are widely available at home improvement centers. Major cracks should be evaluated and repaired by an experienced mason. Sweep or rake leaves and other debris away from the foundation of your house. These materials make appealing natural bedding for mice, insects, and other pests. Check the foundation for cracks and moisture (which attracts carpenter ants). Repair any damage to and then seal the foundation if a professional recommends it.

Windows and doors. Check the caulk around doors and windows and the glazing around windowpanes for gaps. Fill the gaps yourself with exterior-grade caulk.

Deck, stair, and balcony railings. Make sure they have not come loose and repair or replace any that have.

Paved driveways. Check for cracks or holes and have them repaired immediately. Cracks can become large crevices very quickly, especially with the freezing and thawing that can occur in many parts of the country during the late winter and early spring.

Heating and cooling. Make sure any outside heating and cooling units, including propane gas tanks and air-conditioning systems, are unobstructed. Clean the tanks using a sprayer attachment on a garden hose.

GREEN SCENE

My thumb may not be forest green, but during the late spring I am inspired to plant my own beautiful flowers. Sometimes I work with a landscaper, but I really love to go to greenhouses on my own to search for exotic and colorful flowers and shrubs. Beautiful flower beds that punctuate a healthy lawn with established trees also add tremendous value to a home. A neglected lawn sends up a red flag to your neighbors and even future buyers that the rest of the house may not be well maintained, so it is crucial to care for what you've got, if not add to it.

I am not an expert horticulturist by any means, so I recommend consulting a gardening expert or one of the many good gardening books on the market. But here are a few tips you'll want to consider:

- If your lawn is in sad shape (with brown areas, bare patches, crabgrass, weed clumps, and so on), you can renovate it yourself by removing damaged areas (wear gloves to pull weeds and then use a trowel to dig up their stubborn roots) and reseeding with a perennial grass seed. You must cover newly seeded areas with hay and water them regularly until the grass has sprouted. Remove the hay and continue watering the areas until the new seed is well established (this can take a few weeks).

- Fill in perennial beds with annuals during the growing season to add bright color quickly, but consider building up your perennial collection (these are

$ barbara's best bet

TAKE A SLOPE FROM BARE TO BEAUTIFUL

If you have a slope or steep bank that just won't grow grass or is being taken over by crabgrass, cover it with a fast-growing carpet of a ground cover plant such as hens and chicks, ajuga, heather, or creeping thyme. Plants that grow low to the ground stabilize the soil in steep areas and eliminate the need for mowing. They also block out weeds. Evenly space small plants about a foot apart and put wood or pea gravel mulch between them. It typically takes 2 or 3 years for ground covers like these to fill in. And you can add more every year, if you like.

flowers that come up year after year) over time, because perennials are more valuable than annuals. Most perennials should also be divided after a few years, which leaves you with even more plants to spread around, so they are a wonderful investment that keeps on giving. And once a perennial is established, it requires only basic care. Consult your local nursery for advice on the best plants for your area, the conditions they favor (shady, wet, dry, sloped, and so on), and how to care for individual plants. You can't simply walk away from a plant once you have put it in the ground. Don't discount annuals altogether, however—they are a cheap and cheerful way to add color to container gardens and window boxes.

● Maintain your gardens year-round by pulling weeds during the growing season, removing or cutting back dead plants in late fall (rodents love nesting in dead perennials, and dead leaves can also harbor plant diseases), pruning rose bushes and other shrubs, and fertilizing in the fall and spring. Again, because I am not a gardening professional, I seek advice about my precious plants. You should, too.

—— on your own ——

Plant Fall Bulbs for Spring Color!

I love colorful flowers, and spring bulbs offer some amazing hues in the months when spring is trying hard to push away the dreary winter. Planting bulbs is fun, easy, inexpensive, and almost foolproof. Although I am not a serious gardener, I do love planting bulbs in the fall, and it is such a great activity to do with my son. Children love planting bulbs, and when the flowers start to peek through the ground in the spring, you can show your children the wonderful results of their efforts!

September and October are the best months for planting bulbs in most regions because they will have a chance to root before the ground freezes. Some fall choices are daffodils (an especially good variety if you have a deer problem, because they do not eat them), tulips, hyacinths, and snowdrops. The best part is that, come springtime, you'll get great color well before the trees have sprouted leaves or the new shoots of perennials have peeked aboveground. Springtime happens to be one of the most popular home-buying seasons, by the way. Buyers will be seduced by all the gorgeous color in your yard. Bulbs planted casually across a lawn add whimsy to drab springtime lawns, too. By the time early blooming bulbs' leaves have yellowed (meaning it's safe to cut them off without destroying their chance to naturalize and multiply), it's time to mow. Perfect timing. Bulbs also add lots of color to standard flower beds and large planters lining a deck or patio.

How long will it take me? Planting 30 to 40 bulbs should take you a few hours. Planting hundreds of bulbs to get dramatic displays come March or April will require a weekend or two.

How much will it cost? Most garden centers and home improvement centers and even some supermarkets sell high-quality bulbs. You can also find them in mail-order bulb catalogs and online. A bag of 8 or 10 tulips or daffodils can cost between $5 and $10 at the beginning of the planting season (late August or early September). You can also order large quantities in bulk by mail at a great savings, but expect less variety. Sometimes bulbs are marked down later in the season (late October), when there's still plenty of time to plant before the ground freezes. So look for bargains in late fall.

What do I need? Once you have selected the kind of bulbs you want, you need just a few things:

Trowel

Bone meal or other bulb fertilizer

Peat moss or compost if you have clayey soil

Watering can

Mulch

How do I do it?

1. First decide where you want to plant the bulbs. It looks very natural to plant uneven numbers of bulbs together. Some bulbs, like daffodils, naturalize and will multiply year after year. So keep that in mind when planting, too—make sure there is enough room for them to spread (although usually their roots will not interfere with other nearby plants). Planting in drifts is also very pretty, particularly across a lawn or along your driveway. Once you know where you want the bulbs to go, start digging. Bulbs need to be planted fairly deeply so they root well and are protected from freezing and thawing.

2. Excavate the bed to the depth needed. Bulbs should be planted to a depth four times the height of the bulb. If a bulb is 2½ inches high, it should be planted 10 inches deep; a 3-inch-high bulb should be planted 12 inches below the soil surface. A 1-inch bulb can be planted 4 inches deep.

3. Once the hole is dug, add fertilizer according to the package directions—a tablespoon of bone meal, for example, is effective for large daffodils. Mix it into the soil using your trowel. If you have clayey soil, add a handful of peat moss or compost to the soil removed from the bed, which you'll use to cover the bulb. The soil will offer less resistance to the shoots as they grow and provide better drainage for root growth. The bulb itself contains enough food for the flower within it. The extra fertilizer that you provide helps produce larger bulbs for next season.

4. Plant the bulb and fill the hole with the dirt you removed. Using a watering can, water thoroughly.

5. After the ground freezes in late November or early December, cover the bed with 3 inches of mulch to protect it from further freezing and thawing.

———————— ! ————————

We've taken care of the three most important areas of your home—the kitchen, baths, and landscape. But there are many other rooms in your house—bedrooms, family rooms, mudrooms, even hallways and studies—and they're vital to you and to the value of your home, too. I have not forgotten about them, and neither should you. Let's check out what's important about the "living rooms" in your house!

!

CHAPTER 9

Rooms for Living

Your house is so much more than a kitchen, bathroom, and yard. What about family rooms and bedrooms—the areas where you greet friends or seek solace from the demands of the day? These "living" rooms may not have the same functionality as a kitchen or bathroom, but they are important to remember nonetheless. In this chapter, I want to help you make the best use of these spaces.

Adding value and style to the living rooms in your house means maximizing their potential in a way that suits your lifestyle. For example, your four-bedroom house may work better when configured as a three-bedroom with a home office space, or as a two-bedroom with one home gym and a children's playroom. Or, it might mean converting spaces: turning an attic into a bedroom, finishing the basement for a family room, or combining two small bedrooms into a large master suite.

Remember that whatever you do in your home, you should do it for your own and your family's pleasure. Turn an underused dining room into a combination quiet eating area and library. Make the loft at the top of the stairs into a no-TV game room and playroom for you and your children. Transform an empty bedroom into a cozy getaway where soft cushions on a plush sofa, scented candles, and soft music can help you relax at the end of a long day. The special details are what make your house truly memorable and desirable. And if you really love some special feature, someone else will, too. Just keep in mind that any major structural changes you make to these living areas may or may not improve the property's value when it comes time to sell, so I'm here to offer you a few guidelines.

FAMILY GATHERING ROOMS

Every time I travel, I bring back things that remind me of where I have been and what I have learned, whether it's the exotic wood of a picture frame or silk for draperies. Those decorative items often become conversation pieces in my living room, which doesn't serve just one purpose—it's a large, somewhat abstract space that needs to be flexible enough to serve many functions. It's where I greet and entertain guests, gather my family for special occasions, relax, play games, listen to music, and read the newspaper, and Zachary plays with his friends there. I have two double sets of glass sliding doors in my living room that lead straight into the backyard.

The most important shared space in any home is the family or living room, or often today a "great room." In fact, formal living rooms have fallen out of favor in recent years and given way to more informal great rooms that often are connected to the kitchen and dining room. Given a choice, many buyers opt for houses with large, open areas. If you can't add on a great room, look at the floor plan of your house to see if you could "retrofit" one by knocking down walls (and adding support beams to replace load-bearing walls) and combining the family room with the kitchen or dining area. Removing walls to combine areas gives your home a spacious feeling. Removing the ceiling to expose the rafters adds dramatic height to the room—a feature often associated with great rooms. Obviously, all of this requires the work of professionals (check Chapter 5 for more details).

MAKE LARGE SPACES LIVABLE

To make your living, family, or great room more livable and versatile, consider separating large spaces into zones and establishing small environments that can be used for different purposes. For example, in my living room I created a sanctuary in one corner that features a daybed covered with lots of pillows. It's set off from the rest of the space by a latticework screen suspended from the ceiling. Another great way to separate a section of the living room is to have a 6- or 8-inch raised platform in one section for a reading or music nook. Any permanent architectural features like that add a personal stamp with intrinsic value. It should take a carpenter only a couple of days to install a 6 × 8-foot raised area (enough room for a chair, side table, and lamp). And if you feel inspired, it is a DIY project that's not as hard as it seems, especially if you take accurate measurements and get all the wood cut to size at your home center. Materials and labor costs should be around $2,000 if you hire a professional, and maybe even less, depending on where you live. If you do it yourself, material costs average around $300 to $500, a considerable savings.

AROUND THE HEARTH

Upgrading a fireplace is another way of bringing warmth (both literally and in terms of style) to a room, plus it adds great value. Everyone loves the look of a fireplace—even in Florida and California, where they don't see much use! If you have an existing fireplace, how can you make it even better? Consider covering the traditional red brick around the hearth with marble, granite, or handmade tiles. The materials cost would probably be under $100, depending on the tiles you choose. You can do the masonry yourself by following the basic instructions for adding a tile backsplash to your kitchen (see page 132). An antique mantel

comfort zone

USE AREA RUGS
TO DELINEATE ACTIVITY ZONES

Great rooms and big living rooms can be overwhelming to decorate. It took me a while, and I am still working to perfect mine. One easy way to break up the space for different functions without the time and expense of constructing platforms and walls is by using area rugs—even over carpeting. Two or three rugs in coordinating colors but different patterns add texture and vibrancy to a room, as well. Simply place rugs in different areas—one rug can be placed in a TV-watching area, another in the play area, and a third in a place used for quiet relaxation.

or interesting slab of stone or wood changes a plain fireplace into a one-of-a-kind focal point.

If you want to add some fire to your life, consider a zero-clearance fireplace, which is a factory-built fireplace constructed so that it can safely be placed close to combustible materials. Its construction makes it easier to install than a traditional hearth because its venting system is insulated in such a way that it requires less room inside the house. In fact, when you install a zero-clearance fireplace, the contractor does not have to remove the original drywall if it is in good condition. He or she simply sets the unit in place and frames around it. The average cost of these fireplaces ranges from $800 to $1,500 for simple models and can be much more for elaborate or high-tech styles. Count on spending from $300 to $500 (or more; prices vary by region) for labor for installing the fireplace and, if necessary, hooking up the gas line.

A wood-burning stove is another possibility for a home without a fireplace. It must be installed at least 36 inches away from any unprotected combustible wall and placed on a sturdy, noncombustible hearth, such as slate or soapstone. Wood stoves cost from $1,000 to $2,000, depending on their style and size. Installation is extra and can cost $300 to $500.

Gas-powered fireplaces are also an option. The flame is real and so is the warmth, which can be more efficiently dispersed around a room through vents than the heat from a traditional fireplace. Plus, there's none of the mess of firewood and ashes. You don't even have to get up off the couch—gas-powered fireplaces and stoves come with a remote control these days. Expect to pay more than $1,000 for a basic wood or gas stove or fireplace. Keep in mind that whichever firebox you add, your insurance company may need to approve it. That's just one of the many reasons that you'll want a professional to install these items. They are not do-it-yourself jobs.

You can always add a faux fireplace for the architectural detail of an interesting or vintage wood fireplace surround. Take the faux fireplace effect one step further by adding a gel-burning ventless fireplace—a perfect solution if you live in a condo and cannot add a real fireplace. It's also a very nice addition to a bedroom. You can choose from many styles, from ultramodern granite fire "bowls" and hearths to traditional oak or mahogany surrounds. The flame either appears from an opening among or surrounds the ceramic logs. The fuel is actually all-natural, gelatinous alcohol that is 100 percent efficient, soot free, and ecologically sound. Each can of gel burns for 2 to 3 hours. These fireplaces are primarily decorative, but they do create a real flame that's safe and smoke free. The fireplace surround itself, the logs, and a few cans of fuel cost under $1,000. The ceramic log setup alone can be found for around $200, and a case of 24 gel fuel cans costs around $90. You can place them in an existing but non-working fireplace for a realistic effect.

THE RIGHT LIGHT

Adequate lighting is essential in every room, of course, but brightening up large rooms can be especially challenging. There are three kinds of lighting: general, task, and decorative. General lighting, such as overhead and recessed ceiling lights, brightens the entire room. High hats (recessed lighting cans) can be added for between $100 and $250 per light, including materials and labor. It's a good investment, however, since permanent lighting fixtures are selling points. If you have existing general overhead lighting, can you make it better? For example, changing plain overhead light fixtures into shimmering chandeliers or stylish pendants updates a room.

Task lighting brightens areas where you work, read, or play. Sconces placed on either side of a fireplace let you sit and read or do handiwork without disturbing others in the room with bright general lighting. Plus, sconces add style to a room. Of course, lamps placed next to chairs and couches also make reading and hobbies easy to do without the expense of hiring an electrician. Task lighting can also take the form of picture lights above paintings and prints (they are easily retrofitted, and plug-in versions cost less than $50). Up lights and spotlights are very inexpensive and can be placed behind plants to show them off and create interesting shadows against the wall.

Decorative or mood lighting adds personality to a room. Pretty low-voltage lanterns and tiny spotlights add glamour and romance to bedrooms and even living and dining rooms. I have pretty Chinese lanterns installed over the daybed in my living room to further delineate this area as "my" personal space. The price depends on what you buy.

If you have a very large great room, think about having an electrician install outlets in central areas of the floor, which allows you to be much more flexible in placing furniture. For example, lamps can then be placed in the center of the room near sofas and chairs that "float" attractively in the middle of the room. This arrangement is so much more striking and sensible than having furniture pushed up against the walls, wasting the wide-open space in the middle of the room. It's also safer; lamp cords trailing across a room are very easy to trip over.

Finally, install dimmers on all the lights in your living room so it is easy to change the mood from bright and family-friendly to soft and date-time romantic.

go to the pros

INSTALLING A BUILT-IN SPEAKER SYSTEM

I love listening to music while I work, so having an easy way to fill a room with my favorite tunes is a real plus. A built-in system is a great way to do this. It's not difficult for an electrician to retrofit speakers in the ceilings or walls. The speakers can be placed in several places around the room, normally flush with the surface. They can then be painted to match the finish of the wall or ceiling so they virtually disappear. A sound system is a wonderful extra that people often forget about, but once they have it, they love it. It's also one of those features that potential buyers always seem to *ooh* and *aah* over—a great all-around investment.

Who does it?

An audio/video specialist or licensed electrician can install a sound system in your home. A qualified audio system designer or electrician specializing in sound systems can also help you determine the best places for the speakers, much as a lighting designer evaluates a space and the furniture placement within it to create a lighting plan.

How long does it take?

A professional should be able to install a system in less than a day.

How much will it cost?

The kind of equipment you choose has a lot to do with how much you want to spend. You can install a basic sound system in a great room or living and dining area for about $2,000 to $2,500 for materials (six brand-name speakers, amplifier, CD player) and labor—but remember that really high-tech, professional gear is going to cost you a lot more.

What happens?

Balance is the key to great sound, and large rooms may have acoustic challenges. Upholstered furniture, area rugs, and carpets absorb and muffle music volume. Leather furniture and glass tables reflect sound. In a large area with varied furnishings, you may need more than two or three speakers to achieve even coverage and balanced sound levels. So the first thing that happens is that the sound system designer or electrician will help you decide where you want the speakers to go. Speakers installed in the ceiling provide the best dispersion throughout a large space. Experts recommend keeping speakers at least 2 feet from any room boundary, including the edges of the ceiling.

Once you've got the placement set, the electrician will install the speakers and run cables to the equipment, which can be kept on shelves in an existing closet or an entertainment armoire. The entertainment center or closet should measure about 84 inches high by 24 inches wide by 26 inches deep. The components remain out of sight but easy to access. It's not a bad idea to route cables to other locations in the house for future expansion. Just make sure the installer makes a wiring diagram so you know where you can place additional speakers in the future.

BEAUTIFUL BEDROOMS

My bedroom is my sanctuary. I need a special space to be alone, think, rest, and just get away from the world. We all need that! Your bedroom should be a place that's unique to *you*—the furnishings, colors, accessories, and mementos should tell a story about your personality and interests. Creating such a place enriches your life so much. I feel invigorated after a good night's sleep in my bedroom retreat because it's just the way I want it to be, from the colors of my bed linens to the pictures on the walls. Beautiful bedrooms have value, too: The more of them you have, the better, because bedrooms are so simple they can be repurposed to serve as playrooms, offices, craft or sewing rooms, or extra living or family areas. Adding a bedroom is less expensive than adding a bathroom (although not quite as valuable in terms of resale) because it does not usually involve expensive plumbing and electrical work.

ADD A TOUCH OF ROMANCE

My life is so busy and complicated that sometimes even planning a vacation getaway is out of the question. After a hard day of dealing with the myriad demands of modern life, I need to find peace and quiet, and maybe a little romance and fun, in at least one room of our house. Many of us look to the master bedroom for this comfort, which is why the lavish master suite, complete with a spa bathroom and high-tech media system, has become so popular at all levels of the housing market.

I really like the idea of converting part of a closet in the master bedroom into a pantry of sorts, where you can have a small sink and a refrigerator for stashing cold drinks (bottled water perhaps). A shelf can hold bottle openers and glasses. How nice would it be to luxuriate in your room and not have to run to the kitchen to quench your thirst? It should not be too complicated for a plumber to run a water line into a bedroom closet. The remaining space can be sectioned off with a wall and a door and then organized with a system of poles and shelves to hold clothes and shoes. Do-it-yourself closet systems are widely available at home centers. They are very affordable and easy to put together. I used one of these arrangements of poles, baskets, and cubbyholes to organize my own closet, saving literally thousands of dollars over having the closet custom fitted. But at the same time, I added hundreds of dollars in value by transforming my closet. Supersize closets or those with built-in organizational systems pay for themselves (and more!) at resale time. And, they make it so easy to keep clothes, shoes, and accessories organized. With mine, I never have to search for just the right bag or perfect

barbara's best bet

UPDATE CLOSET DOORS

Don't overlook old or troublesome bifold, cheap fiberboard sliding, or unattractive hollow-core closet doors. Replacing old closet doors with newer louvered wooden, decorative, or solid wood doors is a fairly inexpensive project using materials readily available at home improvement centers. Or select mirrored sliders or mirror-fronted traditional closet doors. They give tiny rooms the feeling of more space, which is money in your pocket.

sweater. It's right in front of me, in my pantry/closet. No one ever seems to have enough storage space, so if you can, install one of these systems to increase your bedroom's worth.

go to the pros

ADD FRENCH DOORS AND A BALCONY TO YOUR MASTER BEDROOM

One way of adding a touch of resortlike luxury to a master bedroom is by placing a private balcony off a second-story room or a patio off a ground-floor suite. It's great to be able to fling open the door and step outside on a beautiful morning or enjoy a cocktail with someone special on your private veranda. Who needs a vacation?

This permanent fixture will pay you back fivefold in value, comfort, and enjoyment. A pair of French doors leading out to your private paradise brings even more light into the room, while pretty adjustable window coverings, such as floor-to-ceiling shades, add privacy when you need it. It's an upgrade you find in a lot of new houses these days, too, so adding them is a feature that is sure to be appreciated when you are ready to sell.

Who does it?

A professional carpenter or a general contractor experienced in deck construction

How long does it take?

The amount of time it takes to construct a deck or balcony depends on how big and elaborate it is. You can expect the builder to spend 2 to 3 days digging and pouring footings and erecting posts, beams, and joists and another installing the decking and railings. He or she will spend 1 more day cutting the hole for the door, building a door frame, and completing the installation. So all in all it can take up to 2 weeks, or longer, depending on the design.

How much will it cost?

Depending on how large and elaborate you want your deck to be, and where you live, it can cost anywhere from $10,000 and up. But it's so worth it.

What happens?

If your bedroom is on the second floor, the deck will likely be supported by posts that run into the ground or by a cantilever system. Either way, your architect will file a structural plan because you'll need to get a building permit before work begins. The contractor will pull the permit and start working. Check local building codes, regulations, and zoning restrictions. Deck footings, spans, and deck railings over slopes must conform to specific standards. The location of property lines and easements also might reduce your options, as will any deed restrictions and the location of a septic tank.

Consider the placement of the balcony, too. The layout of your room dictates to a large degree where you can put doors. You may have to move electrical or cable wiring when cutting a hole in a wall to accommodate a door. You may only have room for a single French door, depending on the size of your room.

Since this is a private balcony, not a deck where you will hold large barbecues, you don't have to build a huge structure. You want a space large enough to accommodate a chaise lounge and a table and two chairs. A minimum space of 5 × 6 feet allows two people to sit and relax beside a table. A 12 × 12-foot deck gives you enough space for a daybed and a table with two chairs but is not so large that it would overpower the room or the house.

Construction specifics depend largely on the local building codes, but in general most decks should have sturdy concrete footings that extend into the ground below the frost line. The contractor will dig holes to 6 inches below the frost line, or whatever depth your local building code calls for. Then he or she will pour a few inches of gravel or crushed rock into each hole, set an 8-inch-diameter fiberboard or cardboard pier form on top of the loose fill, then level and plumb the form and fill it with concrete. While the concrete is still wet, he or she will stick a post anchor into the concrete.

If you are able to support the deck with a system of large brackets attached to the house, the contractor should follow local codes to ensure stability and strength. If your bedroom overlooks the roof of a lower section of your house, the building inspector can tell you if local code allows you to build a deck on top of the roof and if so, what the necessary building specifications are. The building inspector should visit the site a few times during construction to track and approve progress. Listen to the inspector and be friendly. He or she is your ally and will ensure that the builder does a good job and follows local building requirements.

If your master bedroom is on the ground floor, consider placing a private patio outside French doors. Depending on your skill level and the condition of the ground, this could be a do-it-yourself project accomplished in a couple of weekends. If the ground is sloped or the terrain is rocky, you may need a landscaper to move earth, level the ground, and set pavers or flagstones. For added privacy, consider adding a privacy fence or hedge around the area.

—— on your own ——

Turn a Closet into an Office

Do you ever find yourself sitting cross-legged on your bed writing last-minute memos to the boss or catching up on some research you didn't have time to read at the office? Working in your bedroom is not conducive to banishing the busy day, but it may be unavoidable if space is limited. That's especially true in small condos or cottages. Why not retain the restful quality of your bedroom and get your work done when you need to by relegating your home office to a closet? It helps keep your work out of sight when it's not in use—just shut the doors at the end of a work session. Simple premade, precut shelves bought at the home improvement center and installed above either a desktop supported by two two-drawer file cabinets or a ready-made desk will make a fine workspace.

How long will it take me? Once you gather all of your materials, it should take you a weekend to complete the transformation. If electrical work needs to be done ahead of time, it's an easy job that should take an electrician only about an hour.

How much will it cost? Depending on the electrician's hourly rate and how many general and/or dedicated outlets you need, it will cost $75 to $150. The materials can be bought for about $300, but you can certainly spend more than that if you want a custom-made desk, for example.

What do I need?

Tape measure

File cabinets and a ¾-inch-thick plywood desktop, cut at the home improvement center to fit the depth of the cabinets and the width of the closet opening, or a ready-made desk in any style, as long as it fits the closet

Two or three premade, prefinished 12-inch-deep shelves cut to the width of your desk

Stud finder

Pencil

Two or three decorative shelf brackets (plus the screws and anchors) for each shelf

Power drill

Screwdriver

Extra storage devices to suit your needs: small bookshelves to mount at either end of the closet, storage containers and pretty storage boxes to stack on shelves

Desk lamp

Wastepaper basket

How do I do it?

1. Measure the height, depth, and width of the entire closet space. You will need to choose file cabinets, or even a ready-made desk, that will fit comfortably in the space and not inhibit the movement of the doors. It's easiest to install this system in a closet with a 48-inch-wide opening and bifold doors. If your closet has sliding doors, you will have to replace them with bifold doors—an easy procedure that can be accomplished by following the door manufacturer's instructions.

2. Remove the pole in the closet, but leave the uppermost shelf if there is one. You can use this to store items you do not use every day.

3. You will also need an electrical outlet in your "office" so you can have light and run a computer or other electronics. If the closet is already wired, an electrician can easily install an outlet. If it is not, he or she can wire the closet and tie the new outlet in to the room's existing wiring. Either way, you should have this taken care of before you begin "construction" of your new office.

4. Paint the walls of the closet in a color that coordinates with the walls of the bedroom. Closets are often painted white, but this is your chance to make the space feel like a real room, and painting is an easy way to accomplish this.

5. Install the shelves under the existing shelf and centered within the closet opening, which is where you will place your desk.

6. Using a stud finder or a tape measure (studs are usually located every 16 inches on center), locate the wall studs in the area where you want to place the shelves and mark them with a pencil. To be secure, shelves must be attached to the wall studs, especially if you plan on storing papers and books on them. If you must attach the shelves between studs, be sure to use the appropriate wall anchors and do not exceed the manufacturer's recommended weight limit. Use the tallest item you plan on storing on your shelves to gauge the amount of space you need between shelves and then, using a tape measure, mark the height for the next shelf with a pencil.

7. Attach approximately one shelf bracket for every 16 inches of shelf span, depending on the weight of the items you plan on storing. The heavier the items, the more brackets you'll need.

8. Lay the shelves on top of the brackets.

9. Place the file cabinets and desktop or the ready-made desk in the closet.

10. If there is space on the side walls of the closet, put small, ready-made bookshelves there or stack storage containers filled with off-season clothes or extra office supplies.

11. Place a lamp on the desktop and plug in your equipment. Fill the shelves with your office supplies, books, and other necessary materials. Place a wastepaper basket by your new desk.

12. Get to work . . . or close the doors, relax, and celebrate your accomplishment!

KIDS' ROOMS AND TEENAGERS' TERRITORIES

The best way to upgrade a child's or teen's bedroom is by adding on a bathroom (see Chapter 7 for more details). Any time you can add a bathroom to a home it adds value, but an extra bath is a real benefit when it helps to alleviate the wear and tear on a family bathroom as children grow into active teens and busy young adults! Do not be discouraged if adding a bathroom is not an option, either because of budgetary constraints or because the board of the condo or townhouse association you are in does not allow for such construction. There are other ways to improve a young person's bedroom.

Paint is great, of course, but be careful—murals and other unusual treatments can take away value. The good news is that if you or your child falls in love with a special mural or paint treatment, it can be easily covered with a coat or two of neutral-colored paint when it comes time to put the house on the market. It's important to get children involved in decorating their rooms—let them choose their favorite colors and artwork. All of these things are removable. If bright purple walls make them happy, why not let them pick out the color and help you paint? They will feel so much more connected to you, your home, and their rooms, and they might even keep their rooms neat if they have a say in how they are decorated.

Permanent storage solutions are the most important feature you can add to family bedrooms. Children's and teens' collections of stuff—clothes, sneakers, games, toys, sporting and electronic equipment—always seem to be growing. Freestanding bookcases are fine, but built-ins add dollar value to a home, especially in bedrooms. You can create a custom built-in look with stock bookshelves by attaching them to the wall with screws (this is safer for children's rooms, too, since there is much less of a chance that the shelves will topple over), especially when you install them symmetrically on either side of a window. A tall shelving unit can be pressed into service as a room divider by attaching it to one wall and the floor with screws. The back of the shelf can be painted or covered with bead-board paneling or even wallpaper or fabric. Or, attach two bookcases back-to-back with screws to divide a room and double the storage space. A lower bookcase of, say, 3 or 4 feet tall can serve as a low divider between twin beds in a shared bedroom. Use your imagination—bookshelves are so affordable and adapt to being all kinds of architectural features in a room.

on your own

Install a Ceiling Fan with a Light Fixture

A beautiful and functional addition to any room in the house is a combination ceiling fan and lighting fixture. Fans don't just add charm and cool breezes, they actually make heating and cooling more efficient. They move hot air around a room in the winter and cool off a hot room in summer, extending for just a little longer the amount of time you do not have to turn on the air-conditioning. They are great in any room but are particularly nice for children's rooms, especially if your son or daughter spends a lot of time playing and doing homework there. It adds another layer of comfort.

How long will it take me? Just a couple of hours

How much will it cost? It depends on the price of the fan—there are so many choices these days that you can spend anywhere from $75 to $500. Home improvement centers always have new styles, ranging from traditional to modern. You will be surprised by what's available. I have seen a tropical-themed fan with blades that look like palm leaves and ultramodern, sleek stainless steel versions, as well as the traditional painted wood styles.

What do I need? Aside from a friend or family member to help you, you need just a few items:

Ceiling fan with light kit

Screwdriver

Wire nuts (usually included in the fan kit)

Electrical tape

How do I do it?

1. The first thing you need to do is select a fan in a style and size that suits your room. For a small room, such as a 10 × 12-foot bedroom, a 36-inch-diameter fan is fine. For a larger room, such as a 15 × 20-foot great room or living room, a fan with a 52-inch span will be more effective.

2. Turn off the electricity at the service panel. As an additional safety precaution, place a sign on the service panel indicating that work is in progress so that someone doesn't inadvertently turn the power back on while you're working.

3. Remove the old lighting fixture.

4. Follow the fan manufacturer's instructions for installation. Here's what you can expect: Attach the fan's mounting bracket to the outlet box in the ceiling using the screws and lock washers provided.

5. Pull the electrical wires in the ceiling through the center hole of the bracket.

6. Study the wiring diagrams and existing wiring before you begin hooking up the fan. In most kits, the black wire is the "hot" wire for the fan and the blue wire is the "hot" wire for the light kit. The green wire

is the ground. Check the manufacturer's instructions to be certain, however.

7. Ask a friend or family member to help support the fan while you install it, because they can be fairly heavy.

8. Attach the canopy to the housing and carefully pull the wires through to make the connection.

9. Be sure to cover all the exposed wire connections with wire nuts before pushing them into the electrical box.

10. Use a screwdriver to install the fan blades, following the manufacturer's instructions.

11. Hook up the light kit. Remove the cover plate and plug.

12. Feed the wires through the hole and attach the cover plate to the light kit, securing the cover tightly so it won't come loose from vibration.

13. Connect the wires according to the manufacturer's instructions. Use wire nuts and electrical tape to make sure that nothing will come loose while the fan is operating.

14. Push the wires into the switch housing and attach the light kit.

15. Install the lightbulbs.

16. Turn the power back on at the service panel and test the fan and light.

BON APPÉTIT: THE DINING ROOM

I love gathering everyone around my long dining room table on holidays. Zach and I have so much fun when my mom and dad, my sister and her family, and assorted friends are all enjoying a meal, laughing, and talking around the table. Even though a lot of people think that dining rooms are kind of old-fashioned, I really like them. They can serve as a place to eat and be used for other activities, too. A dining room is not wasted space, as many people think!

In older and traditionally styled homes, the dining room is set apart from the busy activities of everyday living. In modern homes and apartments, the dining "room" is often an L or alcove off the kitchen or a designated part of a larger living area. That's why we commonly think of the dining room as a place for formal meals and gatherings, and why it's either left to gather dust (because who has time for a fancy dinner party at home anymore?) or transformed into a catchall space for school and work papers, often becoming an impromptu office.

Your dining area can be reclaimed for entertaining and still used for everyday functions with just a little planning and effort. If the dining room is in an area that is attached to or directly off of another living area, such as the kitchen or living room, and is not separated from it by walls, the style and design of the room should blend with the adjacent space. For example, if the dining area is an L off of the living room (a common situation in condos and apartments), consider painting the walls a color that is a slightly different tone of the walls in the living area to distinguish it as a separate space while still relating it to the overall color scheme. Or, if the dining area is simply one end of the living room, paint one entire wall or section of wall near the dining table in a color coordinating with that of the living room to visually separate the space into living and dining zones.

Centering a chandelier or light fixture directly above the table also instantly establishes a dining room feeling in a room that serves dual living and eating functions. An area rug placed under the table also creates the feeling of a room within an open space. Keep the table clear of papers, computers, and other clutter. Invest in a sideboard that can double as storage for such items and for dinner plates and table linens.

If you do have a little-used separate dining room and you want to put what seems like wasted space to good use, consider transforming the room into a dual library/ dining area. During the day and when you are not hosting a party, the room can be used as a place to study and read quietly. With a few storage tricks these two purposes can coexist beautifully. The large dining table can double as a desk, comfortably seating more than one teenager or adult. A sideboard with deep drawers can store papers and pens, a laptop, tableware, and other dining room essentials.

A bench with under-the-seat storage can replace two dining chairs on one side of the table—it will seat more than two people and can discreetly hold even more equipment. If you have room for it, a 4-foot-high, 8-foot-long bookcase can hold your favorite novels, cookbooks, and reference guides (for easy access for homework), and you can display pretty serving pieces, candlesticks, and family photos on the top. A comfortable upholstered chair, small side table, and lamp increase the impression of a library/dining room. What a pleasant environment to eat in! You might even start serving more family meals in the dining room—what a wonderful way to enhance your time at home.

MAKE USE OF FORGOTTEN SPACES

Entryways, hallways, and mudrooms are sometimes overlooked as we improve and change the spaces we spend more time living in. Too often these spaces end up being bland, colorless areas filled with clutter, coats, old papers, and unopened junk mail. It doesn't have to be that way. Here are some tips I love for changing the connecting spaces in our homes from drab to dramatic (and useful).

ENTRYWAYS

It's essential that your entryway be a pleasant first stop for you and your visitors. Simply adding a small table to hold a lamp, a few decorative personal mementos, and a bowl for keys and mail transforms an otherwise forgotten space into something functional and pretty. Consider also adding a stone or tile floor to the entryway—it's so easy to keep clean and stands up to snowy boots and wet umbrellas. If your entryway opens into your living room, as they often do in condos, paint it another color to distinguish it from the other space. If it's super-tiny, add a shelf to the wall to hold a small box for mail and a vase of flowers. A mirror over the shelf lets you check your lipstick before you answer the door for your date. And what about a rack of hooks to hold coats and keys? Even the smallest space can accommodate such thoughtful details.

HALLWAYS

Hallways tend to be neglected because they often are not wide enough to accommodate any furniture and are usually windowless and dark. Line the way with a collection of beautiful mirrors to introduce light and interest. Adding overhead lighting fixtures and wall sconces brings in even more brightness. Widening the entrances to rooms off the hallway brings natural light into the space, too. That's something you can do even in a condo.

MUDROOMS

Backdoor entrances have a tendency to become cluttered, catching everything from shoes and boots to soda bottles and newspapers waiting to be recycled. In my house, Zach and I often leave our beach gear in the mudroom until we've showered and changed from our bathing suits into clean clothes. There are many ways to make your mudroom a comfortable, clutter-free zone. For example, a large covered basket placed right inside the door is a great solution for beach towels on their way to the washing machine and snow-covered hats and mittens destined for the dryer. Add a number of inexpensive stock kitchen cabinets to one wall for storing jackets, gloves, scarves, sports equipment, and school knapsacks. Label the cabinet doors with your children's names to make it extra special. Shelves, cubbyholes, and hooks can make the available space work even harder. A set of stacking recycling bins makes sorting paper and plastics a breeze—and keeps them off the floor. Sturdy hooks are great for hanging up backpacks, jackets, leashes, and keys. A bench or a couple of chairs give you a place to sit down and take off those wet shoes before you track dirt into the rest of the house. A coir mat for wiping off boots and sandy feet is another bonus. If you redo your house's HVAC system or build a new house, be sure to install a small heating vent in the mudroom to help dry wet coats, boots, and mittens.

———— ! ————

If you're feeling overwhelmed at this point, you're not alone.
I wasn't able to make everything in my home just the way I wanted
it right away, either. Making your space as comfortable and stylish
as your vision allows takes more patience and time than money.
You should not be in a big hurry to get things perfect—and I should
practice what I preach! Live in your house and get a feel for it before

jumping into big decorating and renovating projects.
Let the ideas in this chapter percolate in your mind. When I
bought my first house, I focused on redoing the floors and finding a
great mantelpiece for the fireplace. I made those features the focal
points of the room until I had enough money to do more. In fact, even
the living room of the house I live in now just recently came together.
It took me a while to realize the style and feeling that I wanted it
to have for myself, Zachary, and our friends and family.
Whatever room it may be—your bedroom, living room, or dining
room—it can evolve over time as you form design and style ideas
and grow into your home. There's no rush—enjoy the process.

!

Invest in Yourself!

On the Sunday before this book was due to the publisher, I decided to climb a ski mountain in the beautiful Catskills that did not yet have any snow on it. It was a very steep climb, and I eventually began to slow down. PB, my very profound boyfriend at the time, was up ahead, and as I lagged behind, he shouted *"Excelsior!"* to me. I shouted back, panting, "What does that mean?" He hollered back, "It means *ever upward* in Latin." I smiled, took a deep breath, and carried on. I reached the top of the mountain that day.

Reaching your goals and accomplishing things, just like making it to the top of a steep mountain, takes unbelievable persistence. This hill was really a metaphor for everything I had done in business and in life. It was painful walking up the hill, especially because I have a bad knee, but making it to the top was something I really wanted to do. Sometimes reaching your goals is difficult and can even hurt. These endeavors require sacrifice, but you can never lose sight of what you want. You have to reach deep down inside your core and find the strength that will give you the perseverance and determination to reach your goals.

That's what it takes to invest in your home. Living a joyful, beautiful, and comfortable life is a worthy goal, one I hope this book will help you to achieve.

I think real estate is the best investment you can make. Do whatever it takes to stake your claim. I'm certain that doing so will make your life and your children's lives richer and more meaningful.

If I can do it, so can you! *Excelsior!*

The road to success is always under construction.

—Lily Tomlin

!

Index

Underscored page references indicate sidebars.
Boldface references indicate illustrations.